ROUTLEDGE LIBRARY EDITIONS:
POLICE AND POLICING

I0127426

Volume 7

THE BRITISH POLICE

THE BRITISH POLICE

JENIFER M. HART

Routledge
Taylor & Francis Group

LONDON AND NEW YORK

First published in 1951 by George Allen & Unwin Ltd

This edition first published in 2023
by Routledge
4 Park Square, Milton Park, Abingdon, Oxon OX14 4RN

and by Routledge
605 Third Avenue, New York, NY 10158

Routledge is an imprint of the Taylor & Francis Group, an informa business

British Library Cataloguing in Publication Data
A catalogue record for this book is available from the British Library

ISBN: 978-1-032-41114-9 (Set)
ISBN: 978-1-032-41655-7 (Volume 7) (hbk)
ISBN: 978-1-032-41805-6 (Volume 7) (pbk)
ISBN: 978-1-003-35975-3 (Volume 7) (ebk)

DOI: 10.4324/9781003359753

Publisher's Note
The publisher has gone to great lengths to ensure the quality of this reprint but points out that some imperfections in the original copies may be apparent.

Disclaimer
The publisher has made every effort to trace copyright holders and would welcome correspondence from those they have been unable to trace.

THE BRITISH POLICE

by

J. M. HART

M.A.

——

GEORGE ALLEN & UNWIN LTD
Museum Street London

PRINTED IN GREAT BRITAIN
in 11-point Fournier type
BY THE WHITEFRIARS PRESS LTD.,
LONDON AND TONBRIDGE

Introduction

MOST books on local government say little about the police, and
most books on the police say little about its government. But the
administration of the police is of interest both because it is in some
ways unique, and because many of the problems it raises, for
example the proper spheres for central and local control, and the
ideal size of the unit of administration, are common to other fields.
Moreover a certain historical sentimentality attributing almost
magical powers to the unarmed British constable has blurred some
accounts of the British police, and there is a danger lest, in con-
trasting our police with that of Hitler's Germany or Stalin's Russia,
we fail to criticise what we should. To guard against this is not
always easy, for much has necessarily to be kept secret; but there
is no reason why we should not all know more than we do about
our police.

Much of this book is therefore descriptive, but comment has been
included wherever possible. It starts with a general picture of the
structure of the police service to-day. This is followed by two
historical chapters. To many the slow development of the British
police service is one of the most interesting aspects of the subject,
illustrating as it does certain dominant political ideas, but in a book
of this scope the historical side must be brief, and concerned mainly
with throwing light on the present. The ground covered cursorily
in chapter I is dealt with in greater detail in the chapters on central
and local control. There follow chapters on the Metropolitan police
force; policewomen, emphasising particularly their early chequered
history; the topical questions of recruitment, promotion and training; and Scotland. All the previous chapters deal only with England
and Wales, though much of what is said, except the figures in
chapters I to VII, in fact applies to Scotland too. The chapter on
Scotland contains a brief historical account of the development of
the Scottish police and draws attention to the main differences
between the government and administration of the police in England and Wales on the one hand and Scotland on the other. In the
concluding chapter an attempt is made to assess the value, sometimes

exaggerated, of local control of the police, and the relations between the police and the public are discussed.

I have used the term 'Home Secretary' to denote the Minister chiefly concerned with the police in England and Wales, though his correct title is 'the Secretary of State for the Home Department' and he is normally exercising powers which are conferred on 'one of His Majesty's Principal Secretaries of State'. At times I have referred to 'the Home Office' and not to 'the Home Secretary', but too much should not be read into a necessarily arbitrary use of these terms. Strictly speaking 'Chief Officer of Police' means the head of any police force whether he is known as a Chief Constable or as a Commissioner, but I have sometimes preferred the more familiar 'Chief Constable' even where 'Chief Officer' would have been correct.

It is hoped this book will be of use to persons interested in local and central government and public administration, and to members of police forces, British and foreign; and it is, I think, sufficiently free of technicalities to be of interest also to the general reader, and particularly to those who are concerned with the liberty of the subject or who wish to understand and improve the administration of one of the services for which they pay in rates and taxes.

I have not included a bibliography, for the main works and official publications are referred to in the text. An interesting report —the second part of the Oaksey Committee's report on Police Conditions of Service—was issued just as I was going to press. It has not therefore been possible to do more than draw attention to its recommendations on the subjects discussed here, and the interested reader is referred to the report itself.

In writing this book, I have received invaluable help and advice from many, and to all of them I acknowledge my indebtedness and express my gratitude.

J. M. H.

Oxford,
January, 1950.

CONTENTS

PAGE

INTRODUCTION   v

I. *The Present Structure of the Police Service*   1
Police Forces
Police Authorities
The Central Authority
Police Officers
The Office of Constable
Other Constabularies and Enforcement Officers
The Police Federation
The Police Council

II. *Historical Background: to* 1919   22
Before the 19th Century
The Police at the Beginning of the 19th Century
The County and Borough Police Act, 1856
More Policemen—Fewer Forces
Exchequer Grant
Pay and Conditions of Service
The Growth of Representative Machinery and the
    Police Strikes

III. *Recent History:* 1919–1949   45
Reforms
Pay and Conditions of Service
Recent Increases in Pay
The Failure to Amalgamate between the Wars
The Second World War:
        (i) Preparations and Man Power
        (ii) Regional Organisation
        (iii) Amalgamations
        (iv) Control of Police Forces under the Defence
            Regulations
The Police Act, 1946, and Post-war Amalgamations

IV. *Central Control*   69
The Home Secretary's Regulations
Disciplinary Appeals
Inspection
Financial Control
Parliamentary Control
Centrally Run Services
Other Contacts and Controls

V. *The Rôle of the Local Authority*   94
Some Limitations to Central Control
Police Authorities and Chief Constables
Police Authorities and Local Authorities
Assistance from Local Authority Officials
Control of the Police by the Justices
Complaints against the Police
Reform of Police Authorities

PAGE

VI. *The Metropolitan Police Force*   113
      Distinctive Characteristics
      The Senior Officers
      National and Imperial Services
      Finance
      Limits on the Home Secretary's Control
      Parliamentary Control
      Municipal Control
      Amalgamation with the City of London Force
      Conclusion

VII. *Policewomen*   132
      Early History
      1920–1929
      Attestation as Constables
      1929–1939
      Pay and Conditions of Service
      1939–1949
      Equal Pay
      Conclusion

VIII. *Recruitment, Training and Promotion*   152
      The Discretion to Recruit
      The Rate of Recruitment
      The Training of Recruits
      Promotion
      Promotion Rates
      The Origins of Chief Constables
      The Hendon Experiment and the New Police College

IX. *Scotland*   168
      History
      Present Organisation of the Scottish Police and
         Differences from England

X. *Conclusions*   180
      Local Control
      Nationalisation
      The Police and the Public
      The 'Police State'

APPENDIX   189

INDEX   190

CHAPTER I

The Present Structure
of the Police Service

WHATEVER may be the virtues of the British police service, unity and homogeneity in organisation are not among them. Few generalisations therefore are useful in this sphere and the police can only be understood by a relatively detailed study of a number of aspects from which its irregular and complex structure can be viewed. At the outset it is important to grasp that the service is constituted of three parties: police forces, police authorities, and the central authority.

Police Forces

Many people think there is only one police force in this country, and this, they imagine, is run from Scotland Yard. Such is the influence of detective fiction. They are astonished when told there are 129 separate, independent forces in England and Wales alone.* They would have been even more astonished in 1939, when there were 183. No police force has authority throughout the country. Policemen are attested as constables, and have police powers, only for a certain area—the area for which their force is responsible (e.g. county or borough) and neighbouring districts. Provincial police forces, it is true, sometimes ask for the assistance of Scotland Yard in difficult cases, murder cases in particular, but Scotland Yard, or more correctly the Metropolitan police force, does not take any action in provincial cases unless invited to do so, and has no authority over other forces.

The forces vary greatly in size, though not, it is true, as much as in the 19th century when there were several 'forces' consisting of one man; and there is no tidy and symmetrical structure. The largest is the Metropolitan police force, which has an authorised

* This is the figure for 1949. By the end of 1950 there will certainly be two, and probably seven, fewer forces as a result of amalgamations.

strength of nearly 20,000. Next comes Lancashire with 2,800. There are nine other forces of over 1,000; 21 in the 500 to 1,000 range; 29 between 250 and 500; and 69 with less than 250 members. Twelve of these have less than 100 members; the smallest (Rutland) has 25.

It may be objected that these variations in size do not affect the legal position: that the central authority—the Secretary of State—stands in the same legal relationship towards a police authority which maintains a force of 25 men as he does towards a police authority with a force of 2,500 men. This is true; but it is unrealistic to consider the legal apart from the practical position. Powers are of no use unless they can be exercised, and in fact the size and wealth of the unit at times affects its relations with the central authority. The 129 forces must not therefore be thought of as 129 identical units all standing in practice in exactly the same relation to the centre. Moreover the largest of them, the Metropolitan police force, although legally far more closely controlled by the Home Secretary than the other forces, is in fact extremely independent.

With certain exceptions, the areas for which police forces are responsible are the areas of counties and county boroughs. The main exceptions are as follows:

(i) The Metropolitan police force which covers not only the area of the County of London, but also that of the County of Middlesex, parts of the surrounding counties, and three county boroughs. In other words it acts in an area with a radius of about 15 miles from Charing Cross, except for the City of London, which maintains a separate force.

(ii) Some counties which have combined with neighbouring counties to maintain a single force.

(iii) Some county boroughs which have made arrangements to be policed by the county force, and others which have combined with the county force to maintain a single force.

Looked at from another point of view, the position in 1949 can be described as follows. Of the 62 administrative counties, only 49 maintain separate police forces, that is forces which police only the area of the county. Of the 83 county boroughs, 71 maintain separate police forces. (Of the 12 which do not, 10 have never had a force of their own: three of these are in the Metropolitan police district and seven have always had arrangements to be policed by the county force; the remaining two have until recently policed themselves.) There are also six combined forces which each police more than one county or county borough. If to these are added the Metropolitan and City of London forces, and one non-county borough (Cambridge) which has a force of its own, the total of 129 forces is obtained. There are thus fewer forces than there are counties and county boroughs (145).

Police Authorities

Each force has a police authority—a kind of governing body. In the counties the police authority is a Standing Joint Committee composed of representatives of the county council and the county justices of the peace, in equal numbers. The size of these Standing Joint Committees is not laid down by statute: the justices and county councillors are to settle the number between them. If they cannot agree, the Home Secretary is to issue directions. He has seldom had to do this. Standing Joint Committees vary in size considerably, not always in proportion to the size of the force or of the area for which they are responsible. Some do not have more than a dozen members; others have over thirty. Nor is there any statutory provision regarding the length of office of members of these Standing Joint Committees. The usual practice is for the committee to be re-elected every third year after a new county council has been appointed.

In the boroughs, the police authority is a committee of the borough council, known as the Watch Committee. A Watch Committee may not be composed of more than one-third of the members of the council together with the mayor who is *ex officio* a member. The average Watch Committee is smaller than the average Standing Joint Committee, and the variations in size in Watch Committees bear a closer relation to the size of the area for which they are responsible. Most Watch Committees are elected annually, though there is no statutory requirement to this effect.

In the case of combined police authorities, the police authority is composed of such representatives of the constituent areas as are prescribed in the scheme under which they combine. In the schemes so far made, the representatives are elected by the police authorities existing before the initiation of the scheme, except in one case where the borough members of the combined police authority are elected by the borough council and not by the Watch Committee. Some of the schemes prescribe that a Standing Joint Committee in selecting its representatives shall select justices as well as county councillors in equal numbers, which are stated in the scheme; other schemes leave the Standing Joint Committee to select justices or county councillors as they see fit. The members of combined police authorities normally hold office for three years.

The police authority for the Metropolitan police district is the Secretary of State for the Home Department—not the London County Council or the Metropolitan borough councils or a committee of the councils whose areas are policed by the Metropolitan police force. In the City of London which, as already stated, maintains its own force, like a small island in a big sea, the police authority is the Common Council of the City, that is the body corresponding most closely to the town council elsewhere. In fact, as the Common Council, with over 200 members, is so big, police matters are normally delegated to a standing police committee.

It is difficult to describe in a few general words the part played by provincial police authorities in administering the police and to say what exactly are their functions and powers. They have, it is true, certain statutory powers and duties, but the part they in practice play and the exact distribution of powers between police authorities, Chief Constables, and the Home Secretary, is not susceptible of a very precise description. It is sometimes said that police authorities are concerned with general policy. In so far as this means that they do not determine such things as who should be arrested, it is true. But it is not a very illuminating description of their functions: for on the one hand many issues of general policy—such as whether there should be an increase in pay—are determined by the Home Secretary, albeit after consultation with representatives of police authorities and others; and on the other hand police authorities often determine questions affecting one particular man, e.g. the amount of his pension, or what disciplinary action to take against him.

Broadly speaking, outside the Metropolitan police district, police authorities are concerned with maintaining and financing their forces, and not with their day to day running, or, to put it another way, not with the executive or technical control of the men. Subject to the approval of the Home Secretary, they determine the size of the force and the numbers in each rank. They are responsible for police buildings. They grant allowances and pensions subject to the relevant acts and regulations, and they have a certain discretion in connection with some conditions of service.

The police authority appoints the Chief Officer of Police, who is known in the provinces as the Chief Constable, subject to the approval of the Home Secretary, except in the case of the City of London where the appointment is subject to the approval of the King. In the boroughs, the police authority (the Watch Committee) has the power to appoint, promote and dismiss members of the force, and is the disciplinary authority. In the counties, the Chief Constable and not the police authority has the power to appoint, promote and dismiss, and he is the disciplinary authority. Where the police authority is a combined one, sometimes it has the powers of a Standing Joint Committee and sometimes of a Watch Committee, according to which kind of police authority preponderates in the area. In the City of London, the Chief Officer (the Commissioner) and not the Common Council appoints, promotes and dismisses, and is the disciplinary authority.

Because of these differences in the powers of police authorities, it is sometimes said that there are five types of force in England and Wales, viz. county forces, borough forces, combined forces, the Metropolitan police force, and the City of London force. One can usefully classify the forces in this way for certain purposes, e.g. when treating the matter historically or when describing the constitution of police authorities and to some extent the appointment, promotion and dismissal of police officers; but there are few other matters in respect of which one can say that something different happens in each type of force. In particular, apart from a few differences due to local Acts of Parliament, the powers and duties of a police officer towards the public are the same whatever the type of force he belongs to.

The Central Authority

If the local police authorities maintained adequate and efficient forces without advice and financial aid from the centre, the Government would no doubt be prepared to leave them an entirely free hand, as it does not exercise control in order to interfere with the executive functions of the police, e.g. to order arrests. For a short time in the 19th century, the county forces were largely and the borough forces were entirely independent of the central government, but the country was not policed as efficiently as the Government thought desirable and it therefore took powers in 1856 to inspect the forces and to make a contribution towards their cost if they were satisfactorily maintained. The Home Secretary—the Minister primarily concerned with the maintenance of the peace— also makes regulations with regard to the conditions of service (pay, discipline, promotion, clothing, etc.) of the police, and the Home Office has for some time acted as a clearing house of information and a reservoir of experience drawn from all over the country. This emboldens it to issue general instructions and advice on a wide variety of matters concerned with the administration of the police. The Home Secretary thus exercises a general controlling and co-ordinating authority over the police of England and Wales. He is not required by statute to do so, but the Government is, of course, vitally interested in seeing that the country is properly policed. The responsibility for peace and order may therefore be said to be shared between the local police authorities and the Home Secretary. Some responsibility also rests with the magistrates, but nowadays they seldom exercise their powers in this regard.

The Home Secretary is assisted in his surveillance of the police by His Majesty's Inspectors of Constabulary. They are technically appointed by the King as their title implies, but in effect they are appointed by the Home Secretary. There are in 1949 five such Inspectors, and one Assistant Inspector who is a woman. From the time when they were first appointed in 1856 until 1945, the number of inspectors was limited by statute to three, and the number actually employed at any one time was often less. Since the passing of the Police (H.M. Inspectors of Constabulary) Act, 1945, the King may appoint as many as a Secretary of State with the consent of the Treasury may from time to time determine. In introducing the second reading of the Bill, the Home Secretary said that he had no intention of making an increase 'of a dramatic order' in the number of inspectors, or of changing the existing structure of the police service with its separate forces; but he wanted to be able to strengthen the inspectorate so that it could deal with the many complex problems of the police in the post-war years.

Inspectors of Constabulary are usually persons who have served in a police force, normally as Chief Constables. For various reasons it has not been the practice to appoint young men to the staff of the inspectorate, as, say, assistant inspectors, and to train them up for the post of inspector as is done in some services. A new departure was, however, made with the appointment in 1946 of a police staff officer whose duty was to advise the Inspectors on matters connected with policewomen; this staff officer has now been made an assistant inspector. The important thing in appointing Inspectors is to secure persons, who, whilst having a thorough knowledge of police work in all its aspects, can yet detach themselves sufficiently from the service so as to be able to criticise it where necessary from the standpoint of an objective outsider. It is also, of course, desirable to appoint persons who, whilst being experienced, have not lost the vigour of youth.

The cost of the police, which was once borne entirely by the rates, is now borne in broadly equal shares by the Exchequer and the rates. The expenses of each force are charged in the first instance to the police fund of the force, but the Exchequer makes to each police authority a grant of 50 per cent. of their approved expenditure on police purposes. The Metropolitan police fund receives a special contribution of £100,000 a year (in addition to the normal Exchequer grant of 50 per cent. of approved expenditure), for the imperial and national functions which fall on the police of the capital. The City of London police fund on the other hand receives less than half its expenses from the Exchequer: the 50 per cent. grant less the product of a rate of 4d. in the £. This special arrangement was not, as might be thought, made at the request of the City Corporation in order to put it in a position of special independence. On the contrary, when the Exchequer started paying grants towards the City force in 1919, the Corporation asked for a grant-in-aid amounting to half its expenditure on the police, but this was not agreed to by the Government which presumably thought the Corporation was rich enough to contribute more than the usual half.

The total cost of maintaining the police service, including pensioners, in England and Wales during the financial year 1949-50 was nearly £47 million, of which £24 million was borne by the Exchequer. The corresponding figures for 1948-49 were £42 million and £21½ million. The estimated figures for 1950–51 are: total cost, £50½ million; Exchequer share, £26 million.

Police Officers

Police forces are, it need hardly be said, composed of police officers. The term 'officer' is not here used, and is seldom used by the police, to denote those in the higher ranks as contrasted with those in the other ranks; it includes all policemen and women. There were in England and Wales in 1949 59,000 police officers of whom about 1,000 were women. Police authorities were authorised to employ 71,000, but could not recruit the numbers they desired. This gives an overall average of about 600 inhabitants for each authorised police officer and about 720 inhabitants for each actual police officer. There is now no statutory limit, as there was at one time, to the number of police officers who may be appointed in proportion to the population and the ratio varies considerably from place to place—from over 1,000 inhabitants per policeman* in a few counties to five (night) inhabitants per policeman* in the City of London. The average* for rural areas (790) is higher than the average* for towns (599, excluding London). Leaving aside the City of London where the circumstances are exceptional, the Metropolitan police district, with 422 inhabitants per policeman*, is almost the most densely policed area in the country.

There are different kinds of police officers. The great majority are what is known in the service as 'regular' police officers, that is, they usually serve for 25 years or more and retire on pension. In normal times they are the only policemen and women serving. They are the 59,000 referred to above. During the war temporary police (men and women) were engaged for the emergency. Most of the men were enrolled in the Police War Reserve, and most of the women in the Women's Auxiliary Police Corps. These bodies were disbanded at the end of 1948.

In addition, in each force there is provision for a body of men known as the First Police Reserve which is composed almost entirely of police pensioners or men with previous police experience, who are prepared to give whole-time, paid service to a particular force in an emergency, whether national or local. During the war members of the First Police Reserve served continuously, but they

* Authorised.

have now mostly reverted to their normal position as a reserve. There is no statutory provision authorising the maintenance of a First Police Reserve, though model conditions of service have been drawn up by the Home Office. As a second line of reserve, though one which is not of secondary importance, police forces have the Special Constabulary. Apart from the war-time expedient of engaging some special constables for whole-time, paid service, the Special Constabulary consists of volunteers who perform short periods of duty, without remuneration, in the spare time from their normal occupations. About 18,000 men were thus regularly employed in 1949. They are used mainly for such work as controlling crowds at processions, races, meetings, etc., or during civil disturbances. Much of the ancillary work in police offices is performed by persons known as 'civilian employees', though police officers are also civilians in the sense that they are not members of the armed forces. The duties performed by these civilian employees include clerical, typing and telephone work, and the maintenance of cars. They are not members of police forces.

Before 1829, there were virtually no police ranks. Persons known as high or head constables existed, it is true, in most areas and exercised some slender supervision over the petty or parish constables; but there was nothing like the elaborate hierarchy that we know to-day, fashioned on a military model (or so it struck Maitland in 1888) with regular grades of subordination—chief constables, superintendents, inspectors, sergeants and constables. These ranks were instituted gradually throughout the 19th century, and since 1920 the titles have been prescribed by the Home Secretary's regulations. Intermediate ranks such as assistant chief constable, chief superintendent, chief inspector may be adopted with the Home Secretary's approval. The ranks in the Metropolitan police force are rather different. All forces do not have officers in all ranks, though most of them, since the abolition of the smaller forces in 1947, have at least one representative in each of the main ranks. But these ranks have for the most part only an administrative, as distinct from a legal, significance: a policeman's rank has very little influence on his legal relation with the public, and the responsibility of superior officers consists ultimately in ensuring that their subordinates properly discharge the duties of their office as constables.

The Office of Constable

While in the internal organisation of a force 'constable' is the
name for a man in the lowest rank, all police officers (except the
Commissioners) are constables, that is, they hold the office of
constable. This applies to all the different categories referred to
above—regulars, auxiliaries (except some of the women auxiliaries),
first police reservists, and, of course, special constables. The Commissioner and Assistant Commissioners of Police of the Metropolis
and the Commissioner of Police for the City of London are justices
of the peace, not constables—a curious arrangement in some ways,
reflecting much history, but one which enables the Commissioners
to swear in their own constables.

The law requires that every person who is appointed a member
of a police force shall be sworn in as a constable before a justice of
the peace, and it is usually held that a man only becomes a member
of a police force when he has been so sworn in. The Acts requiring
members of police forces to be sworn in as constables (the Metropolitan Police Act, 1829, the County Police Act, 1839, and the
Municipal Corporations Act, 1882) do not prescribe the exact words
of the oath; what seems to have been intended was that men on
appointment to a police force should make the declaration which a
constable normally made on appointment. It had been the practice
for constables to take an oath before a justice of the peace for many
hundreds of years. The words of the oath were prescribed for special
constables in the Special Constables Act, 1831, and most forces have
used and still use that form or something very much to the same
effect for all their officers. The form of that oath is as follows:

'I A.B. do swear, that I will well and truly serve our Sovereign
Lord the King in the Office of Special Constable for the Parish (or
Township) of . . ., without Favour or Affection, Malice or Ill-will;
and that I will to the best of my Power cause the Peace to be kept
and preserved, and prevent all offences against the Persons and
Properties of His Majesty's Subjects; and that while I continue to
hold the said Office I will to the best of my skill and knowledge
discharge all the Duties thereof faithfully according to Law. So help
me God.' Since 1868, a declaration has been substituted for an oath.

The fact that a police officer makes a declaration that he will
serve the King, and not, for instance, the police authority or the

Home Secretary, is important. It results in his being an officer of the Crown and not a servant of the police authority. This does not mean (as some might think) that he is given orders by the King or by the Home Secretary on his behalf, but that he is an independent holder of a public office whose duty it is to enforce the law of the land. McCardie J. held in *Fisher* v. *Oldham Corporation* (1930) that if a police officer arrested a man for a serious felony and the Watch Committee passed a resolution directing that the felon should be released, the resolution would be of no value; the plain duty of the police officer would be to disregard the resolution, and, moreover, the Chief Constable would have a duty to consider whether an information should not at once be made against members of the Watch Committee for a conspiracy to obstruct the course of criminal justice; if local authorities were to be liable in such a case as this for acts of the police in respect of felons and misdemeanants, then it would indeed be a serious matter and it would entitle them to demand that they ought to have a full measure of control over the arrest and prosecution of offenders. To give any such control would, this Judge considered, involve a grave and most dangerous constitutional change.

It follows that a constable is personally liable in respect of any mistaken or wrongful action on his part except where he is acting in pursuance of a magistrate's warrant. Even if he was obeying the orders of his police authority, they would not be liable. This might in certain circumstances fall hardly on an aggrieved person. His case lies against the individual policeman concerned, but the policeman may be unable to pay the damages awarded by the court. In such a case the police authority would in fact probably make the plaintiff an *ex gratia* payment, whilst denying all liability, but they are not obliged to do so. It might also be suggested that the principle enunciated in *Fisher* v. *Oldham* would encourage police officers to be timid in performing their duties. Even if this is so, it is a small price to pay for freedom from interference by the police authority with the enforcement of the law. The position is, however, in certain respects curious: the police are officers of the Crown, controlled to some extent by police authorities, and in the case of the provincial police paid in law by county and borough councils.

Nor are superior officers of police responsible for the wrongful acts of their subordinates, except where the acts complained of were performed by their express orders. The liability of the police thus differs from that of members of the armed forces. It would be misleading, however, to suggest that a policeman is not subject to the general supervision of, and to directions from, his superior officers, or that this supervision is not of importance; but for a great part of the time he is not acting under specific instructions and must rely on his own discretion and knowledge of the law.

Most modern writers and official spokesmen about the police stress the antiquity of the office of constable. Thus Sir J. Moylan, in 'The Police of Britain' (1946), states (p. 12): 'The authority which clothes them [the British police] is that of the office of constable with its unbroken lineage of 700 years.' And a Home Office witness in 1920 before the Baird Committee on the Employment of Women on police duties said, 'To be a member of a police force is merely a modern statutory thing; the status of a constable goes back into dim antiquity'. This emphasis on the antiquity of the office of constable is in some ways strange, as many of its previous holders have not approximated very closely to the modern British conception of the perfect constable. Moreover, it seems inconsistent to emphasise, as is often done, both the genius of Peel in providing that his new police should be constables, and that the secret of law enforcement was suddenly discovered in 1829, the new police being something very different from anything that had gone before. The more important fact is that a constable is not the servant of the police authority and cannot be given orders by them.

Many of those who 'write up' the office of constable stress that he has few powers which the ordinary person has not and that he is only doing for payment what everyone could do if they had the time and inclination. This is said to be one of the things which distinguishes the Anglo-Saxon police system from those of countries which inherited the Roman system and, more important to-day, from the totalitarian systems of the continent of Europe. Some currency was given to this theory by the following passage in the Report of the Desborough Committee of 1919 on the Police Service:

'We consider it important also to bear in mind that the constable, even in the execution of his duty for the preservation of the peace, acts not as an agent of the Government, exercising powers derived from that fact, but as a citizen, representing the rest of the community, and exercising powers which, at any rate in their elements, are possessed by all citizens alike. The citizen is still bound, at the direction of a Magistrate, or on the appeal of a constable, to take his part in the preservation of the peace and suppression of disorder, and in this country the whole power of the constable rests on the support, both moral and physical, of his fellow citizens.'

This surely overstates the case. A constable has many powers which other men have not; powers of arrest for instance: he alone can arrest persons found committing certain offences, and he alone can arrest on suspicion in certain circumstances. 'These [powers] are still important', wrote Maitland in 1885; 'it is mainly because he is a constable, an officer long known to the law, that he whom we call a policeman differs from other men.' Then a constable has certain duties which other men have not: he must under certain statutes accept an offender who is handed over to him by someone else and bring him before a magistrate; if he refuses, he is liable to a penalty. A constable also has certain privileges in order to enable him to carry out his duties more efficiently, e.g. a certain amount of protection against actions for damages, and exemption from jury service.

It is more difficult to say how far the public have confidence in the police because they feel the policeman is only a person who is paid by the community to carry out on its behalf duties which belong to all citizens. The police are certainly popular amongst most sections of the population in England to-day, but not, it would seem, for this reason. Most people probably do not realise the wide powers of arrest they possess; still less do they realise that they have a duty to exercise these powers if they can. The public, therefore, very seldom exercise their powers of arrest, and tend to think that only the policeman has the right to arrest anyone.

Besides what he can do as a constable, the modern policeman can often do things because some authority, usually the local authority, has appointed him an inspector under some statute. Examples of such duties are the inspection of weights and measures, the diseases of animals, food and drugs, explosives, shops. In most or all of these cases the appointing authority is free to employ as inspectors any fit persons, but finds that policemen are the fittest. The 'inspectees', o use a word coined by Maitland, may or may not appreciate that the policeman when making an inspection is acting as an appointed inspector and not as a constable. Some duties the police cannot be required to perform: for instance, that of mayor's attendant, town crier, or the collection of market tolls; these are prohibited by the Home Secretary's regulations.

Other Constabularies and Enforcement Officers

To complete the picture of the police, certain other constabularies must be mentioned.

Some public utility services employ police of their own. The most important of these are the Railway police, the London Docks police, the River Tyne police, and the Manchester Docks police. These policemen are constables, sworn in before justices of the peace, but their duties and powers are limited to the premises and immediate neighbourhoods of their employers. Each of the three Defence Services maintains a small corps of constables mainly to guard their property. These are the War Department Constabulary to guard War Office lands and military places, the Royal Marine Police who are employed chiefly in dockyards, and the Royal Air Force police for R.A.F. establishments. These police do not usually have much official contact with the general public. They are distinct from the Corps of Military Police, the 'Red Caps', and their naval and air force counterparts, who are not constables and are concerned with the observance of military and naval law by members of the armed forces.

During the last decade, another addition has been made to the class of those whose duty it is to enforce the law: various Government Departments, particularly the Board of Trade and the Ministries of Fuel and Power, and Food, have appointed officers to enforce their orders and regulations. Normally this would have been the task of the police, but it was presumably thought that they could not undertake further substantial duties of this kind. There were in 1949 still over 1,000 of these enforcement officers and inspectors, about 85 per cent. of whom were employed by the Ministry of Food. They may work in close collaboration with the police, but they are not constables. In the main they derive their powers from warrants issued under the Defence Regulations, not by the courts, but by certain authorised civil servants. These warrants may relate to a class of undertakings and not merely to one specified undertaking, and therefore give the inspectors greater powers than they could obtain from warrants issued by the ordinary courts. Generally speaking these officers have powers of entry and inspection, and can take samples of what they find, but they have no powers of arrest other than those which are possessed by the ordinary citizen. For the most part these enforcement officers use their powers scrupulously, and criticism which is made of them should often be directed against the law they are enforcing; but the existence of a body of *quasi* police officers entirely outside the ordinary police service is an undesirable development and might become obnoxious. There are many less of them than there were at one time, but it is difficult to see how they can disappear whilst rationing and controls remain: apart from shortage of man power, the ordinary police would probably be reluctant to take over the enforcement of specialised, temporary, and unpopular laws of this kind. It is therefore all the more important to watch the activities of these enforcement officers and to try to ensure, through the courts and otherwise, that they do not exceed their powers and do not resort to undesirable devices to enforce the law.

Thus is England policed.

The Police Federation

Most of the 59,000 police officers in England and Wales have, as one might well imagine, many common problems, although they are members of 129 different forces. They feel the need to discuss and make representations on these problems and they are allowed to do so through the medium of an organisation known as the Police Federation. In the words of the Police Act, 1919, which set up the Federation, it is to enable members of police forces 'to consider and bring to the notice of the police authorities and the Secretary of State all the matters affecting their welfare and efficiency, other than questions of discipline and promotion affecting individuals'. All members of police forces below the rank of superintendent are automatically and without payment members of the Federation, but there is nothing to compel a police officer to play any part in the Federation's work. Police officers above the rank of Inspector cannot join the Federation.

Among all the different types of organisation from trade union to staff association which now exist, the Police Federation is in many respects unique, and it is therefore of interest not only to the student of the police service, but also to the student of the trade union movement. The machinery through which the Federation is to act is prescribed by statute. It consists of Branch Boards, democratically elected by the three lowest ranks in each force, who may sit together or separately, and the usual superstructure of central committees and conferences. Neither members of ranks above inspector, nor Home Office officials, nor Inspectors of Constabulary have a right to attend any of the Federation's meetings. The Home Secretary is normally invited to address the annual conference, but otherwise all meetings of the Federation are confined to its members. The number and duration of the meetings which may be held are limited by statute, though special permission may be obtained for additional meetings.

All officials of the Federation are elected by its members; and their choice is not subject to confirmation by any authority, but the officials must be selected from the police. In any event it would be difficult to appoint an outsider as the Federation has no funds from which it could pay such an official. Members of the Federation are normally entitled to be given leave to attend its meetings and to receive pay and expenses as if they were on police duty. In addition one police officer, but only one, is allowed to spend his whole time on Federation work, and the Exchequer bears all the running expenses. The Federation is thus financed entirely from public funds. The cost to the taxpayer and ratepayer of all its activities is well over £10,000 a year. For some years in the early stages of its existence, the Federation pressed strongly but unsuccessfully for permission to create and maintain a fund from voluntary subscriptions from its members. The Oaksey Committee has now recommended that this should be allowed in order to finance certain additional activities.

But although the Government and the police authorities finance the Federation, they do not, as a condition of giving this aid, or otherwise, seek to control its activities. Any organ of the Federation is free to discuss and make representations on any matter it likes concerning the welfare and efficiency of the service, except questions of discipline and promotion affecting individuals. Welfare is interpreted broadly; it includes pay and all conditions of service, and in fact representations are made on a variety of matters, from the constitution of the Police Council, or requests for more pay, to the need for better bicycle lamps. Questions of welfare have concerned the Federation much more than questions of efficiency, which is unfortunate in some ways.

A Branch Board makes its representations to the Chief Officer or police authority concerned, but it may also make them to the Home Secretary whether or not it has got support from one of the central organs of the Federation. It can thus bring to the attention of the Home Office any matter on which it has not got satisfaction locally. Moreover, Central Committees have a right to a personal hearing from the Home Secretary on matters of importance. There is thus ample machinery for the airing of grievances.

The Police Act, 1919, provides that the Federation and every branch of it shall be entirely independent of and unassociated with any body or person outside the police service. The Act also prohibits a member of a force from being a member of any trade union, or of any association having for its objects, or one of its objects to control or influence the pay, pensions or conditions of service of any police force. The reason for these provisions is obvious, namely the desirability of keeping the police out of politics. There are further restrictions of a similar kind in the Police Regulations. They require that a member of a police force shall at all times abstain from any activity which is likely to interfere with the impartial exercise of his duties, or which is likely to give rise to the impression amongst members of the public that it may so interfere; and that in particular a constable shall not take any active part in politics. A trade union can, it is true, affiliate to the Trade Union Congress without affiliating to a political party, but the T.U.C. concerns itself with many political matters and if the Police Federation were affiliated to Congress, their delegate at the annual conference would be able to express in public his views on political issues and on Government policy. Moreover, if the Federation were affiliated to the T.U.C., Congress might at times be requested to take up with the Federation the action of the police at political meetings or demonstrations. There might also be difficulties in connection with strikes as the police have sometimes to intervene in disturbances arising out of trade disputes in which the unions are involved. Altogether it would obviously be most undesirable to allow the Federation to affiliate to the T.U.C., for the police should at all costs appear, and indeed be, absolutely impartial. The result of the prohibition is inevitably that the police are isolated from workers in other fields. They cannot, except privately, discuss and compare their conditions of service with members of other professions, and they cannot receive any assistance from outside in putting their case to the authorities. Contact with other workers might help the Federation to see their conditions of service in a better perspective and militate against any tendencies towards narrowness of outlook or sectarianism. But these advantages would by no means offset the great harm which would be done if the police were not strictly excluded from politics. It should be added that the Federation have not asked for an alteration of the law to permit them to affiliate to the T.U.C.

Until recently, the Home Secretary took the view that individual policemen should not approach Members of Parliament on personal or service matters, and that the Federation through its machinery should not lobby or write to M.P.s without permission from the Home Office. There have even been instances of Chief Constables putting policemen on disciplinary charges for writing to M.P.s on service matters, it being an offence under the discipline code for a police officer to communicate to any unauthorised person any matter connected with the force. These restrictions appeared unnecessary to Mr. Herbert Morrison when he was Home Secretary and are no longer enforced. As long as police officers do not divulge to any outside person any matter connected with their work which should be kept secret in the interests of preventing or detecting crime, it would seem right to allow them to make representations to M.P.s or any other person on their conditions of service, provided this does not lead to some outside body, other than Parliament, taking up their case.

On the whole the constitution of the Federation appears to be well suited to a service such as the police, whose activities it is necessary to restrict in certain ways in the interests of discipline and political impartiality. Some members consider it is too much of a 'company union', but it has more freedom in electing its officers and in making representations than many staff associations where the 'boss' takes the chair and pay must not be discussed. As a result of the Federation's activities, many grievances have been remedied and many improvements in conditions of service effected. At one time some police officers thought that if one wished to be looked on favourably by the authorities, one should not be an active member of the Federation. This was unfortunate, especially as it narrowed the field from which the Federation's officers were selected. There was some justification for their fears, but now even the most old-fashioned senior members of the service see the Federation as at least a safety valve, and recent Home Secretaries have frequently pressed new recruits to play an active part in its work. The Federation presented the Oaksey Committee with a formidable list of grievances about the limitations on their activities and obstacles placed in their way. On most of these issues the Committee did not consider the case proved, and apart from their recommendation about funds, they did not suggest any alteration in the constitution or scope of the Federation, though they considered that, subject to the requirements of police discipline and efficiency and the mainten-ance of public confidence, the Federation should be allowed as much freedom as possible to decide the scope of its activities.

There is no statutory provision for organisations to represent the interests of the ranks of superintendent or above, but they are nevertheless allowed to present their collective views on service matters. The superintendents and chief superintendents have one organisation which was set up by the Home Office by administra-tive arrangement, and the chief constables and assistant chief con-stables another, which they set up themselves. The Association of Borough Chief Constables dates from 1896. Unlike the early associations of the lower ranks, it was tolerated by the authorities, although not specifically permitted by statute.

The Police Council

The Police Council is the central consultative body of the police service. It, too, was set up by the Police Act, 1919. It is composed of representatives of police authorities, and of all ranks of the police. The representatives of police authorities and of Chief Officers are selected by the Home Secretary after consultation with the County Councils' Association and Association of Municipal Corporations. The superintendents' organisation nominates its representatives, and the three lower ranks are represented by members of the Joint Central Committee of the Police Federation. The Act of 1919 does not say how many representatives there shall be of each of the bodies concerned and under-representation of various groups has at times been alleged. For some years now the police authorities have had 12 representatives, the Federation nine, the Superintendents three, including one woman, and Chief Officers eight (including two Commissioners). The chair is taken by the Home Secretary or a senior member of the Home Office. Appropriate Home Office officials also attend, together with the Inspectors of Constabulary.

The Police Council has no executive, but only consultative and advisory, functions. The Police Act, 1919, requires that the draft of any regulations which the Home Secretary proposes to make under the Act—as to the pay, conditions of service and other matters affecting police officers—shall be submitted to the Council, and requires him, before making regulations, to consider any representations made by the Council. The Act does not require the Home Secretary to *accept* the Council's advice and it does not therefore prescribe what he is to do if different sections of the Council give him conflicting advice. The Home Secretary is also required to consult the Police Council before making pensions regulations.

It is also provided in the Act of 1919 that the Home Secretary may arrange for the holding of Police Councils for the consideration of general questions affecting the police, at which representatives of the Federation may be invited to meet representatives of police authorities, Chief Officers and superintendents. To-day it seems curious that it was thought necessary to include this in an Act of Parliament: there would have been nothing to prevent the Home Secretary arranging meetings of persons representing various interests in the police either to resolve their difficulties or to advise him. But the statutory provision is understandable in the light of the troubles of the years 1918–1919: it was an effort to set up a piece of conciliatory machinery to bring the two *sides*, as they were then seen, together. In fact the division of opinion is as often between the police officers (Federation and higher ranks) and the police authorities, as between the Federation and the others. But the original conception of the Council is still reflected in its seating arrangements: the representatives of the Federation always sit furthest away from the chairman at a table separated from that of the police authorities and higher ranks. This may be thought a mere detail, but it is one which is regarded by many of the rank and file as symptomatic of the attitude of 'the authorities'.

Meetings of the Council are held whenever there is sufficient business for it to transact. The Home Secretary is not bound to summon it even if this is requested by one of the constituent bodies, except when he proposes to make some regulations; but in fact it is now the practice to consult the Council about any proposal materially affecting police conditions, whether or not an amendment of the regulations is involved. There is normally at least one meeting a year; recently there have been four or five.

For several years the Federation has been critical of the way in which the Police Council functions and has asked that it should be transformed into a kind of Whitley Council, with recourse to arbitration when agreement is not reached on the Council. The recommendations made by the Oaksey Committee, which are summarised in the Appendix, grant the substance of the Federation's request. This will mean a substantial loss of powers for the Home Secretary and involves a change of a fundamental nature.

CHAPTER II

Historical Background:
to 1919

Before the 19th Century

I T may seem to us a matter of course that there is in this country a
body of policemen, highly organised and disciplined, paid to maintain order, detect crime and arrest offenders. But all this is comparatively new: it has existed for only about 100 years; and for some time
before then men were severely puzzled how to maintain order
without endangering personal liberty. There had, of course, for
many centuries been some kind of organisation (if that is not too
grand a word) for apprehending offenders, but it was remarkably
unlike the police service as we know it to-day.

In Anglo-Saxon and early Norman times the unit in what we
should call the police system was not the county, but the hundred
and the township, whose nearest modern equivalents may perhaps
be said to be the rural district and the parish respectively. Both the
hundred and the township had the duty of apprehending criminals
and could be fined for neglecting it. This system of collective
responsibility and collective fining was probably found not to be
altogether satisfactory, and it came therefore to be the practice for
the inhabitants of each township to appoint one of themselves to
take this responsibility on his shoulders for a special time, normally
a year. In Anglo-Saxon times this officer was called by a number of
different names, but in Norman times he was given, at any rate by
the court lawyers, a new name—'constable'. It is not clear why this
happened, but the most probable explanation appears to be that
the Normans required the local official whom they found on the
spot to perform duties (e.g. enrolling men in the militia) which they
associated with the military officers known in France as 'cones-
tables'. But what is of interest from the point of view of the history
of the police is not the origin of the title 'constable', but the organi-

sation that existed for detecting and apprehending offenders. The two questions are not always distinguished.

Besides the constable of the township, who developed into the parish or petty constable, there was also a head or high constable of the hundred, who exercised some superintendence over the parish constable; but his duties were mainly in connection with the militia and his authority over the parish constable declined. Theoretically the head constable had most of the responsibilities of the modern Chief Constable, but in fact he had no power to appoint, control, or dismiss his assistants, and, as the importance of the hundred as an administrative unit declined, his place was gradually taken by the justices of the peace.

From the 12th century, country gentlemen were from time to called upon to help in enforcing the law, a system which was given a statutory basis early in the 14th century, when legislation was passed relating to the officers who afterwards became justices of the peace. At first their authority was simply executive, being limited to suppressing disturbances and apprehending offenders. Then they were given judicial powers and what to-day would be called administrative duties. The sphere of government was gradually enlarged, and as there was no bureaucracy, whatever Parliament wanted done was to be done by justices of the peace, and whatever the justices wanted done fell on the shoulders of the constable. He became the justice's factotum, executing his orders and warrants and arresting offenders. He was also expected to make reports to the justices assembled in Quarter Sessions on offences committed in his district and on the general morality and behaviour of the inhabitants.

The constable was at first elected by his neighbours at the court known as the court leet, a practice which gradually became less democratic as for one reason or another the number of electors diminished. This court, which had a certain criminal jurisdiction over petty offences, was a hundred court, and it was no doubt because the hundred was the responsible unit in the police system that the constable was elected at the court leet. Later the appointment came to be made by the justices in Quarter Sessions. Opinions differ as to how rapidly this change took place, but a later rather than an earlier date seems the most probable, and indeed some courts leet were still appointing constables in the 19th century. But the distinction between the two methods of appointment was probably of little substance, for leet courts were all in the hands of lords of the manor, and justices of the peace were lords of the manor.

It had, however, certainly been the practice long before the 17th century for justices to swear constables in to their office, though it is not known when this became customary. It is sometimes suggested that with the swearing in of constables before justices, who derived their authority from the Crown, local administrative officers were converted into ministerial officers of the Crown, and that this step marks the subordination of local to central government in rural districts. But it seems improbable that the practice of swearing constables in before justices, which was largely formal, altered their relationship or meant that the constables were subject to more directions from the justices than previously. It has, however, been a factor of some constitutional importance, because it led the courts later to lay down that a constable was not a servant of the police authority, but a ministerial officer of the Crown.

The office of parish constable was unpaid, save for certain fees and allowances for expenses. It was also compulsory; and every capable inhabitant of the parish, apart from persons in certain exempted classes such as the clergy, knights, clerks, and women, could be appointed constable. But as the duties of constables increased in volume and perplexity, the office became more and more unpopular. The middle classes in particular regarded it as a waste of their time, and disliked having to assume for a whole year an unpaid, arduous office which might entail enforcing unpopular laws. They therefore took to paying deputies to do the job for them. By the time of the Tudors the paid deputy was fairly common. The deputy had to be approved by the appointing body—court leet or justices—but in spite of this safeguard he tended to be inferior to the original nominee. The practice of appointing deputies led to some extent to the growth of a class of professional constables, as the deputies often went on from year to year, but in spite of this it did not make for efficiency, as the constable elect naturally looked for the cheapest substitute he could find, and the average deputy was therefore a simple, illiterate, poor man who wanted to supplement his income, but who was incapable of coping with the responsible and complicated duties of a constable. For by the 16th century besides the constable's main common law duty of arresting offenders, he had a good many small duties connected with paupers, vagrants, apprentices, wages, working hours, etc. This is another example of Parliament employing for its purposes a pre-existing institution. It is well to remember that Parliament did not create the office of constable, though it has recognised, defined, sometimes amplified, sometimes limited it by statute. This fact has, in the eyes of constitutional historians, surrounded the office with a good deal of traditional sanctity; the fact is certainly of interest, but it seems doubtful whether it shows much more than that the office of constable is older than Parliament, and that men felt a need to preserve the peace before the King felt a need to call a Parliament.

Few structural changes in the organisation of the rural police occurred in the 17th and 18th centuries, apart from the two years (1655–1657) of rule by the military police when the country was divided into 12 districts. The dislocation of the civil machinery of the country during the Civil War was not followed during the Restoration by an overhaul of the police system, which continued in essentials as it always had been, though declining in effectiveness. The Government resorted more and more to offering rewards to thief-catchers, a system which invited abuses, and the maintenance of the peace remained at a low ebb. The moral character and social position of the constable was not improving, indeed it was probably deteriorating, and, as Blackstone said, considering the class of man who commonly acted as constable, it was just as well that he remained in ignorance of the powers which were entrusted to him by the law.

In the towns supplementary assistance had for a long time been provided by watchmen. The system of 'Watch and Ward' was established, or perhaps regularised, by the Statute of Winchester of 1285. This statute required the appointment of a prescribed number of watchmen in all towns to guard the gates. All male inhabitants were liable to serve their turn on the watch without payment. The institution had certain characteristics in common with that of fire-guard officer in the 1939–1945 war. Watchmen were not constables, and one of the duties of constables was to keep a roster of the watchmen, to call them out and to see they were vigilant. By the 18th century a great number of towns had no watchmen, and in those where there were some they were mostly very unsatisfactory. During the 18th century many towns made an effort to reform their policing arrangements by getting local Improvement Acts passed which authorised the appointment of Improvement Commissioners, who were responsible for the scavenging, lighting and paving of the town as well as for its policing.

In London different types of experiment were made. From 1750 onwards magistrates, particularly the Fielding brothers, organised small bodies of paid whole-time constables to act under their directions. The Government took an increasing interest in these reforms and assisted them with money. The most famous of these bodies were those attached to the Bow Street Court.

Various reforms in the policing arrangements of the whole country were advocated during the second half of the 18th century, but no changes of substance were made. It was generally thought that an organised, paid constabulary force would not concern itself only with law breakers, but would interfere with the liberty of law-abiding citizens. Nor was it thought that a body of civilians could prevent or control riots: for this the military were relied on, though they were singularly unsuccessful, not only when faced with serious situations such as the Gordon Riots of 1780.

The Police at the Beginning of the 19th Century

London

In the City of London, the policing arrangements were under the control of the municipal authorities—the Lord Mayor, Aldermen and Common Council. Outside the City, in Westminster and the growing suburbs, the parochial authorities were responsible and the police were appointed by different bodies: vestries, church-wardens, boards of trustees, commissioners, and courts leet. Superimposed on this network, were small bodies of constables under the direction of particular magistrates and the Bow Street patrols for whom the Home Secretary was responsible. There was also a river police which had some official support.

Even if every constable and watchman in London had been efficient, which they were not, it is obvious that the system could not have functioned effectively: no authority, municipal, central, or judicial had any power to co-ordinate the arrangements in the 130 parishes. The magistrates had full control of the constables attached to their courts, but these were few in number and found it impossible to work with the parochial police officers. In some parishes there was no parochial police at all, and in many the numbers employed were grossly inadequate. Moreover, constables and watchmen were paid mainly by fees according to the work they did, a practice which led to many abuses.

No less than six parliamentary committees of enquiry sat between 1770 and 1828 to investigate the state of the police of the Metropolis. Apart from the last one, in 1828, they were mainly appointed as a result of alarm after some particular crime or disturbance, and their recommendations, though by no means comprehensive or radical, were lost sight of as soon as the alarm subsided. It is easy for later generations to be scornful of these timid men who thought that freedom and an effective police system were incompatible, but we must remember that they had heard much of the excesses of the police of the *Ancien Régime* in France and had lived through Napoleonic times and the reign of Fouché. Even the Committee of 1828, of which Sir Robert Peel was a member, admitted that there were serious difficulties to encounter, but it came to the conclusion that determined efforts should be made to effect a decisive change. Its recommendations were implemented in the Metropolitan Police Act of 1829, which strangely enough passed through Parliament without opposition, indeed almost without debate. Two Commissioners, acting under the Home Secretary's directions, were to organise a new force to replace most of the existing agencies, and for the first time the policing of the whole of the Metropolis, except the City of London, was to be in charge of one authority. The area concerned was much the same as that of the County of London to-day.

Some Marxist historian will no doubt one day assert that in reforming the police of London, Peel was the tool of the *bourgeoisie* who wanted their property protected and the working classes prevented from taking action to improve their conditions. This theory will not stand up against the facts: it was the propertied classes who opposed all suggestions of police reform as attacks on personal liberty, and, more prosaically, on grounds of expense. And Peel's motives appear not to have been those which the Marxist analysis would impute: he wanted to mitigate the savagery of the criminal law, and this could not be safely done with an inefficient police. He wanted, it is true, to reduce the amount of crime, but this would have helped the poor as well as the rich, though perhaps not in the same degree; he wanted to reduce the expense to which anyone was put who wished to enforce the law, by having a paid constabulary not dependent on fees; he wanted to take the patronage out of the hands of the parochial authorities and to ensure that the new system was not made 'a job for gentlemen's servants and so forth'. As to quelling mob violence and preventing industrial trouble, this appears to have been much less in Peel's mind than preventing and detecting the more ordinary type of crimes—robberies, larcenies, etc. Moreover, it was generally felt by those who wished to reform the police, that it was most undesirable to call out the military to keep order and that it was preferable for this to be done by the civil police.

At first there was violent opposition to the new force. Complaints were mainly concerned with their arbitrary actions and the expense. The public were given every opportunity to complain to Select Committees of the House of Commons which sat in 1833 and 1834, and every allegation was carefully investigated. The force was exonerated of arbitrary actions except for one incident, and most reasonable people saw what a great improvement the new police was on the old. To those who thought, as many did, that the police could be self-supporting by being paid from the proceeds of fees and licences, the Metropolitan police force appeared expensive, but it was run very economically in its first years, and the Commissioners were ruthless in dismissing unsatisfactory members.

In 1839 an Act was passed making various alterations in the area and organisation of the force. The Metropolitan police district was enlarged to almost its present boundaries and the police agencies still remaining outside the control of the force were merged into it. Members of the force were also given additional powers to assist them in their work.

The Boroughs

The arrangements for policing provincial towns varied considerably from place to place. There were constables in all towns, but they were appointed by different agencies: the court leet, the mayor and aldermen, or the magistrates. By whomever appointed, however, the constable probably came under the supervision of the magistrates in his work more than under that of the Corporation officials or High Constable. His chief duties were to execute the magistrates' orders; he did not watch or patrol the streets as does the constable of to-day, in order to prevent crimes. The constable was paid sometimes from the Corporation out of the rates, sometimes from the contending parties to a dispute. The watch also were appointed and supervised by different agencies, but the most common arrangement, at any rate in the larger towns, was for them to be under the control of Improvement Commissioners, who were distinct from the Corporation.

Much the same defects were to be found as in London. Too many bodies were concerned, and confusion and antagonism resulted. Unless specially authorised, a constable had no powers outside his town. In some towns there was neither day nor night watch, an incredible state of affairs in the light of the amount of crime at that time. It is clear that unprofessional, barely remunerated, part-time peace officers were by the beginning of the 19th century, and indeed earlier, wholly inadequate to prevent and detect crime, maintain public order, and enforce the law. The system had broken down under the strain imposed on it by the growth of population and the conditions of urban life during the Industrial Revolution.

The improved arrangements for policing London threw into relief the defects in the provincial boroughs, and when they were reformed in 1835, the opportunity was taken to try to improve their policing. The Municipal Corporations Act, 1835, therefore required every one of the 178 boroughs to which it applied to appoint a Watch Committee, and the Committee were to appoint a sufficient number of constables, who were to have powers not only within the borough, but in the surrounding area. The cost of the police was to fall entirely on the rates and the Corporations were entrusted with complete control: they had to report certain matters to the Home Secretary, but he had no power to inspect or interfere.

The Counties

The organisation of the police in rural areas was simpler than that of the towns. It was based on the parish, and the only police were parish constables, of whom there were one or more per parish. They were appointed by courts leet or justices, and, as in the towns, were supervised chiefly by the justices. They appear not to have done any preventive work—nor did anyone else—but they found their duties arduous and complex, and then as now we hear the complaint that the increase in statutes imposed a heavy burden on the constabulary. At a time of crisis, the justices might swear in extra constables. They had done this for many years, but in 1831 an Act laid down the procedure and regularised the practice. The most common use of 'special' constables, as they were known, was at elections and during civil disturbances.

It is obvious that by the 19th century the parish was far too small a unit for the administration of the rural police. A parish constable's authority ended at the frontier of his parish and the system would have been hopeless even if all constables had been full-time paid officials chosen with the utmost care. In fairness to the parish constable it must be said that to have done his duty properly would have required a terrific sacrifice of time and labour for little pay, and that it would have been asking much to have expected an untrained and little educated village constable, who received almost no guidance from superior officers, to have coped with the increase of crime which was taking place and to have kept abreast with the changing methods and increased mobility of law breakers. Moreover, many parts of the criminal law needed amending, and it is never easy to enforce a law which appears too harsh either to the general public or to those whose duty it is to enforce it. But whatever excuses can be made on his behalf, the fact remains that he was more often than not grossly inefficient. This may have ensured that there was little interference with certain important liberties of the subject, though even so irregularities were by no means unknown.

In 1836, the Government appointed a Royal Commission of three persons, one of whom was Edwin Chadwick, the secretary of the new Poor Law Commissioners, to consider the best means of establishing a rural constabulary. The Commission, which reported in 1839, was anxious to avoid patronage in appointments and saw many advantages in the police not being recruited locally. They therefore recommended that the counties of England and Wales should be policed by a force whose members would be appointed, organised and managed by the Metropolitan Commissioners who would assign contingents to the different localities for employment under the orders of the justices in Quarter Sessions. The force would be under the ultimate control of Parliament. The Government would bear one-quarter of the cost, the rates the remaining three-quarters. This scheme met with much opposition and was not adopted by the Government. Indeed the Government do not seem to have been immediately persuaded that it was necessary to have paid, permanent policemen in all rural areas whatever the method of control. They were, however, stirred into action by Chartist disorders. A Bill was introduced late in the session which in just over a month became the County Police Act, 1839.

This Act enabled the justices to maintain a paid police force, either for the whole county or for any particular division of it. The numbers were not to exceed one for every 1,000 inhabitants. The members of the force were not to engage in other paid work. Except where they were appointed for one division of a county only, the constables had authority in adjoining counties as well as in their own. The cost was to be borne by the general county rate. The Act gave the Home Secretary far wider powers of control over the administration of the county police than he had over the borough police, a difference which can probably be accounted for by the long-standing independence and power of the Corporations. For, besides approving the numbers to be employed in the counties, he was empowered to make rules for the government, pay, etc., of the constables and his approval was necessary to the appointment of the Chief Constable. Rules for the county police were made in 1839.

The County and Borough Police Act, 1856

It is misleading to think of the years 1835 and 1839 as witnessing sudden and fundamental changes in the policing of the boroughs and counties respectively throughout England and Wales. Police reform outside London was gradual, patchy and unspectacular compared with what happened in the Metropolis. Perhaps this is why the policing of the provinces came in for less criticism than that of London.

By 1856 the forces in the largest towns were on the whole big enough and fairly efficient, but the policing of many middle-sized towns and of most of the smallest ones still left much to be desired. In a few places no attempt whatsoever appears to have been made to comply with the police sections of the Municipal Corporations Act, 1835. It was, of course, difficult, if not impossible, for the smallest places to maintain efficient 'forces', as their size did not warrant the employment of more than two or three men. The Act of 1835 required every borough to which it applied, however small, to maintain a force: the choice in 1835 lay between this and leaving the smaller boroughs unpoliced, as there were no forces in the surrounding counties with whom they could have been required to consolidate. In any event the independence and pride of the boroughs were such that they would no doubt have successfully resisted any such requirement. It is true that an Act of 1840 permitted any borough to consolidate its police with that of the surrounding county, but little advantage was taken of this. Looking back, it is clear that England would have been more efficiently policed in the 19th and indeed in the 20th century if the county police had been reformed before the borough police and if the smallest boroughs had never had their own forces: having once given them authority to create their own forces, it was difficult to take it away.

In the rural areas, the results of the Act of 1839 were disappointing to those who had hoped for much from it. By 1856, police forces existed in 24 counties and in parts of seven others, but in 20 counties no action had been taken. The main deterrent against adopting the new Act was the expense anticipated: protagonists of the new 'preventive' police usually maintained that in the long run the new system, although involving paid full-time officers, was not more costly than the old one as it led to a decrease in crime, but it was difficult to convince the ratepayers of this. Where the Act of 1839 had been adopted, improvements in the prevention and detection of crime followed, though even the new forces left much to be desired. Stimulated by a critical report of a Select Committee of the House of Commons, the Government in 1854 made some half-hearted efforts to introduce reforming legislation, but it was not until 1856 that the law was altered.

The County and Borough Police Act, 1856, required the justices to establish a paid police force for the whole of each county. Crown Inspectors of Constabulary were to visit the county and borough forces and to report on their efficiency to the Home Secretary. The Government would provide one-quarter of the cost of the pay and clothing of every county and borough force which was certified by an Inspector to be efficient in numbers and discipline, except in the case of boroughs with less than 5,000 inhabitants: they could consolidate with the counties for police purposes or pay for their own forces. The majority preferred survival to support. The Bill was attacked in the most virulent and exaggerated terms, amusing to read now: it took away the right of self-government and destroyed local institutions which had existed since Alfred; by requiring Chief Constables to make annual reports to the Home Secretary as to the state of crime, it was no better than the continental spy system; the aim of the Government was simply to maintain the game laws, as, if it were not for these laws, a rural police would not be required; the boroughs were perfectly well policed; the Town Councils were models of efficiency; it was more economical to rely on military aid in an emergency than to maintain a large number of police for an occasional riot, strike or contested election; nobody was asking the Government for money; the proposal to give a Chief Constable control over his men might have originated from an Austrian or a Russian nobleman; indeed it was the most un-English measure ever seen and seemed more fitted for Naples than for England. The Home Secretary made certain concessions to the boroughs: in particular he dropped a proposal that he should have power to make rules for the borough forces on the same matters as he could already for the counties, provided fees to borough policemen were abolished and the Home Office could obtain the statistics it required. Although Government Inspectors were at this time not unknown in other fields, it is perhaps not to be wondered at that Inspectors of police were viewed with alarm. Nevertheless, the opposition of the boroughs to all proposals in the Bill which affected them in any way seems to us to-day somewhat unreasonable. But even as amended the Bill made important changes: for the first time the whole of England was to be policed, and machinery and sanctions were provided to see that the law was complied with.

The first Inspectors of Constabulary were far from being ogres: on the contrary they positively apologised for the suggestions they made; and this in spite of the fact that they found numerous defects, especially in the boroughs. Each force acted in its own way, which made co-operation difficult, even when tried. Many forces were too small; discipline and supervision were poor; in some forces no records were kept; and in many the cells were unfit for human beings. On the whole the Inspectors' advice was welcomed and taken, though a few forces were so suspicious of interference that they declined to accept any financial assistance from the Government. This did not, however, save them from inspection.

Improvements were gradually effected, as can be seen from the following figures:

Year	No. of forces reported inefficient
1857	120
1860	78
1870	56
1875	38
1885	25
1890	Nil

More Policemen—Fewer Forces

The total number of policemen in the country increased during the second half of the 19th and 20th centuries, as one might expect in view of the growth in population, but the proportion of policemen to population also rose as the following figures show.

Year	Full-time police		Inhabitants per police officer		
	1 Provinces	2 London	3 Provinces	4 London	5 Average
1830	—	3,350	—	455	—
1840	—	4,840	—	443	—
1857	12,000	6,640	1,365	446	1,040
1861	13,000	7,230	1,300	441	999
1871	15,860	10,350	1,187	375	867
1881	19,480	12,020	1,091	402	828
1891	23,070	15,890	1,014	355	734
1901	27,360	16,900	949	396	738
1911	31,780	19,270	907	381	710
1921	35,700	20,240	852	369	677
1931	36,530	20,850	869	393	696
1939	40,850	19,650	777	417	660
1949	42,900	16,360	803	506	721

Notes: (a) Columns 2 and 4 relate to the Metropolitan and City of London police forces, except for the year 1830, when the City is not included.
(b) All figures relate to police officers (men and women) actually employed, not to the sometimes larger number of officers authorised.

It is disheartening that we apparently need, or at any rate sponsor, more police relative to the population than our forefathers. We should aim at managing with fewer and fewer. In a completely law-abiding community one would not need any police except for calamities arising from physical causes and for a few tasks such as controlling crowds and traffic, and we should save nearly £50 million a year.

At the same time as the number of police rose, the number of forces fell, though slowly, as the following figures show.

NUMBER OF FORCES

Year	Counties	Boroughs	Total, including Metropolitan and City of London
1857	59	178	239
1860	58	166	226
1888	57	172	231
1889	57	124	183
1900	58	137	197
1910	60	128	190
1920	60	129	191
1930	60	121	183
1939	60	121	183
1943	56	101	159
1947	56	73	131
1949	55	72	129

Legislation affecting the unit of police administration was not introduced until 1877. The Municipal Corporations (New Charters) Act of that year provided that no scheme for the incorporation of a borough might provide for the formation of a separate police force for the borough unless the population exceeded 20,000. In 1888 the Local Government Act provided that the police forces of all boroughs with a population of less than 10,000 in 1881 should be merged with the county force. The Inspectors seized every possible opportunity to try to get the smaller forces to merge in their larger neighbours, but very few voluntary amalgamations took place, and there were in 1919 still 49 forces with less than 50 men. There was no legislation affecting the size of police forces or the unit of police administration between 1888 and 1919, indeed until 1946, except certain war-time measures, though this was constantly recommended. The industrial troubles of the years

1909–1913 showed up the weaknesses of the small forces which had constantly to try to borrow men from neighbouring forces, but there was no crisis sufficiently serious to embolden the Government to incur the wrath of the smaller boroughs by taking their police forces from them.

Exchequer Grant

From the start the Exchequer bore some of the cost of the Metropolitan police, but it was not until 1856 that it contributed to the cost of the provincial forces. The inefficient forces, of course, received no grant, and it was not until 1890 when many of the smaller boroughs had disappeared that every force in the country, except the City of London which did not want assistance, was in receipt of Exchequer grant. Between 1890 and 1919 the Exchequer contribution was not finally withheld from any police authority, but the threat to withhold was frequently used to enforce the Home Secretary's will.

The Act of 1856 permitted the Government to contribute only to the pay and clothing of the provincial police. All other expenditure, the most substantial items of which were buildings and pensions, was borne wholly by the local rates. From 1890 onwards the Government also contributed to the pension fund of each force if the fund was properly administered. The limitation of the grant to these items safeguarded the Exchequer, but it restricted the range of matters on which the Government could bring successful pressure on police authorities.

The Police (Expenses) Act, 1874, removed the maximum limit to police grant of one-quarter of expenditure, and under the general scheme for the relief of local taxation which was introduced in that year, the Exchequer contribution towards the police was increased to one-half of the cost of pay and clothing. This applied to the Metropolitan police as well as to the provincial forces. In 1879, the Exchequer grant amounted to nearly £1,210,000, which was more than twice what it was in 1870, viz. £465,000. Even this was almost twice what it was in 1857, the first year grant was paid.

It is interesting to contrast these developments in England with what was happening in France at the same time. There the central government managed to maintain an absolute control over the entire police of the country through the Prefect of Police of Paris, the Prefects of the departments and the Mayors of the Communes, without contributing to the cost, except in the case of Paris and a few other places. With these exceptions, the entire police of France was at the end of the 19th century paid out of local funds, unassisted by the central government, but it was far more closely controlled by the Government than was the English provincial police.

The conditions which had to be satisfied before grant was paid were also altered from time to time. Under the Act of 1856, a force had only to be efficient in point of numbers and discipline to receive assistance. From 1890 onwards the management and efficiency of the force had also to be satisfactory before grant could be paid. But even these conditions were not wide enough for some purposes: they did not, for instance, enable the Home Office to bring pressure to bear upon police authorities who had not made plans to co-operate with other forces in an emergency. Moreover, the system was cumbrous because the Home Secretary could not deprive an authority of part of the grant: it was all or nothing.

In 1888 the direct grant in aid of expenditure on the police was abolished and assistance from the Exchequer was provided in a different way. Half the cost of the pay and clothing of the police was made a charge on the Exchequer Contribution Accounts of counties and boroughs, the accounts being made up from the proceeds of certain taxes, known as 'assigned revenues'. Whereas previously Exchequer grant had increased with any growth in approved expenditure, after 1888 the amount of Government assistance was independent of the expenditure of police authorities. It was soon obvious that the system was not satisfactory, and in 1901 the majority of the Royal Commission on Local Taxation recommended that it should be replaced by a grant to each police authority equal to one-half of the net cost of the police, including the cost of police stations. This recommendation was not acted on. A similar recommendation was made by the Departmental Committee on Imperial and Local Taxation which reported in 1914. This would have meant a substantial increase in Exchequer grant. The scheme was embodied in a Bill in 1914, but was not proceeded with because of the war. It was not until 1918 that the Home Office made a supplementary grant from the Exchequer which relieved the rates of nearly half the cost of the police.

Even then the grant arrangements remained very complicated.

The Desborough Committee of 1919 did not recommend the abolition of the assigned revenues system, nor of the separate contributions to the pension funds; it only suggested that the direct supplementary grant which started in 1918 should be increased so as to
cover at least half the net cost of the police. It was not until 1929
that the system was simplified; in that year the statutory grants in
respect of police expenditure and the system of formal certificates
of efficiency were abolished. This did not mean that forces were
paid grant whether they were efficient or not; on the contrary it
made it easier to withhold grant, as the direct non-statutory grant
was not tied to any certificates or conditions except those laid down
in the Home Secretary's own rules.

Pay and Conditions of Service

One of the chief obstacles to the employment of full-time paid
policemen had been fear of the cost. When they were finally
appointed, therefore, the Home Secretary, Watch Committees and
justices did all they could to keep expenditure as low as possible.

Broadly speaking, men in the lowest ranks of the police service
during the 19th and early 20th centuries were paid at the same or
only a slightly higher rate than unskilled manual workers. But this
statement needs many qualifications as police pay varied considerably from force to force. No scales of pay were prescribed by the
Home Secretary for borough policemen until 1919. Certain scales
were prescribed for the counties from 1839 onwards, but they left
room for considerable divergences. When revised in 1886, the
Home Secretary's rules permitted seven different scales for constables, and other scales could be adopted with his approval. The
scales prescribed in 1886 were not altered until 1919, though war
bonuses were paid during the first world war.

The absence of uniform rates of pay for any of the ranks led to
difficulties, and during most of the 19th century wastage was high.
As early as 1857 the Inspectors recommended that the rates of pay
should be uniform, and from time to time commented on their low-
ness, but uniform scales for the lower ranks for all types of force
were not introduced until 1919, by when the differences between
the forces had become greater than ever. Moreover, during the
19th and early 20th centuries the pay of Chief Constables increased
proportionately much faster than that of constables, and Chief

Constables, especially in counties, were more commonly provided with free houses or allowances in lieu and other extra emoluments than were the lower ranks. There appears, however, to have been even more dissatisfaction over superannuation than pay until the reforms of 1890, when minimum pensions of a reasonable amount were made obligatory.

The Growth of Representative Machinery and the Police Strikes

Before 1919 there was no machinery through which policemen in different forces could raise with the Home Secretary any questions about their pay or conditions of service. For those matters which were wholly at the discretion of the local police authority—e.g. pay in borough forces—it may be thought that there would have been little purpose in any such machinery, but if the central government had been more aware than it was of the grievances of many policemen, it might have brought pressure to bear on those police authorities where pay and conditions of service were at their worst, thus perhaps averting some of the troubles of the years 1918–1919. In any event, representative machinery would have been useful from the men's point of view in connection with such of their conditions as were determined centrally—by legislation or otherwise.

Nor was there in most forces any machinery through which policemen could raise with their own police authority—either individually or collectively—questions about their pay and conditions: these were settled by the authority without any consultation with members of the force other than the Chief Constable. A man could make an individual complaint to his superior officer, but he would usually be chary of doing so as he might be regarded as insubordinate and reprimanded or punished. Collective or joint complaints were regarded by many of those in authority as dangerous: they augured mutiny; they would have made the maintenance of discipline impossible. Discipline itself was often administered in an arbitrary way by Watch Committees and Chief Constables; no discipline code was laid down centrally; standards varied widely from place to place, and there was no right of appeal to any person, tribunal or court against any punishment, including dismissal. The right of appeal to the Home Secretary against the most severe

punishments which was instituted in 1927 was the first measure of
this kind for the police.

Though many policemen were from an early date dissatisfied
with their pay and conditions of service, those in forces outside
London were so scattered that joint action was difficult. The first
effort to get some organisation to represent the views of the rank
and file was made by the Metropolitan police force in 1872. In that
year meetings of constables were held in London to discuss grievances. These led to the setting up of a representative committee to
formulate the case for increased pay, better pensions and a reduction
of hours of duty. The authorities tolerated the committee as long
as it appeared to be temporary, but when the organiser tried to
make it permanent, he was dismissed for insubordination. As a
protest, 180 men of the Metropolitan police force refused duty.
Suspensions, dismissals and reinstatements followed.

A similar incident occurred in 1890, and from then onwards there
was constant agitation in the police service for the 'right to confer',
as it was known. The earliest organisation for this purpose was
formed at the beginning of the 20th century. It became known as
the Metropolitan Police Union and later the National Union of
Police and Prison Officers. The Home Office and police authorities
intimated that those who joined, or tried to persuade others to join,
the Union would be liable to dismissal. Nevertheless, the membership of the Union increased, and by 1917 was quite considerable.
Some branches of the Union affiliated themselves to Trades or
Labour Councils, and the Union itself was affiliated to the Trade
Union Congress. The view has been held that other trade unions
were responsible for the formation of the Police Union, hoping
thereby to prevent the use of the police in connection with strikes.
The other unions were no doubt sympathetic to the formation of a
union of police officers, and may have played some part in its foundation, but it is not difficult to see why the police themselves should
have wanted an organisation of this kind at that time, and have felt
it essential to get some backing from the established trade unions.
For during the years 1914–1918, there was much discontent in the
police. Pay, which had never been high, did not keep pace with the
rise in the cost of living, and such increases as were made did not
for some time count towards pensions. The police contrasted their
emoluments with those of munition workers and not unnaturally

became extremely disgruntled. Differences in pay and allowance from force to force became greater than ever, which created further difficulties. Police duties were hard and hours long. It was, however, recognised by all except a few extremists that an impossible situation would be created if policemen belonged to an organisation which claimed for its members the right to strike in certain circumstances and which was liable to have pressure put upon it by other organisations, political and industrial.

For a few years the Union was active in certain areas, overtly or clandestinely, and claimed a 95 per cent. membership in certain forces. In August, 1918, the pro-unionists in the Metropolitan force decided the time had come to compel recognition and to gain more support from the men by means of a sudden and successful strike. On a constable being dismissed for joining the Union, they presented demands for increased pay one day and struck the next. The strike, which lasted from 29th to 31st August, 1918, involved nearly the whole of the London police, but did not spread to the provinces. The dispute was settled for the time being by the reinstatement of the dismissed constable, certain concessions on pay and pensions, and the recognition of an authorised organisation—entirely distinct from the Union—to represent the men. None of the strikers was dismissed: the authorities not unnaturally thought it essential to get the Metropolitan police force going again at once at such a critical stage in the war. The settlement, however, was only temporary. The new organisation, which consisted of representative boards formed according to a scheme drawn up by the Commissioner, was not very popular; the Union was still in existence, and there was discontent both in the Metropolitan and in provincial forces. In March, 1919, the Government appointed the Desborough Committee to review *inter alia* the conditions of service, rates of pay and pensions of all members of police forces in Great Britain. Within three months the Committee issued its first report recommending considerable improvements in pay and conditions of service. These were generally acceptable to the police service, but the Union, nevertheless, called a general strike in July, 1919, and secured a considerable amount of support. The strike was against the clause in the Police Bill (which was then before Parliament) making it illegal for the police to join a Union other than the Federation established by the Bill. Over 1,000 men of the Metropolitan police force went on strike. They were joined the next day by men from six other police forces. Altogether 2,400 police out of a total of 60,000 withheld their services. The situation was at its most serious in the Liverpool area where severe rioting and looting took place, and the military and many special constables were called in to restore order. The strikers did not achieve their object: the Government did not alter the provisions of the Bill to which they objected.

One cannot help being less sympathetic to the strikers of 1919 than to those of the year before. By July, 1919, the police had secured or been promised considerable improvements in pay and conditions of service, and there were obvious and overwhelmingly strong objections to allowing their organisation to be affiliated to other unions. On the other hand, it may be said for the men who went on strike that it was never very clear what was settled in 1918. Many policemen thought that they had been conceded a right to a Union and that the representative boards were only a temporary arrangement to be superseded at the end of the war by a Union. After the settlement of 1918, no official action was taken against policemen who joined the Union even where membership was a breach of regulations. The Union, therefore, thought it had been partially recognised. The negotiations had been between the Prime Minister, the Home Secretary and representatives of the Metropolitan police force, but not the Commissioner, and this fact led to difficulties, as the terms of the settlement were in dispute. Nor was the Commissioner made more sympathetic to the Union when it advanced such incredible proposals as that the representative board should have access to all his papers, and power to compel the attendance before it of any member of the force—including the Commissioner. On the other hand, many policemen felt and with justification that the Union had been instrumental in getting them better conditions of service and that they must be loyal to the comrades who had worked hard for them.

But whilst one does not feel much sympathy for the strikers of 1919, one cannot help regarding some of the strictures which were passed on them as unduly severe. 'Men who in the interests of their fellow citizens', wrote an Inspector of Constabulary in 1920, 'have been trained to exercise self-restraint and patience may well be expected to exercise these qualities where their personal interests are affected'. They had 'departed from their solemnly plighted obligation' and were no longer 'honourable men of their word'. The oath of a constable was a promise 'any honest man could make without sacrifice of his manly independence', but a man who broke this oath by going on strike could no longer be believed in the witness box. To the men who attributed their improved pay and conditions in some measure to their agitation, it is unlikely that the strikes appeared, as they did to H.M. Inspector, as 'an episode which has brought pain and grief to everyone who has the welfare of the police service at heart.' If consultative boards had been set up in all forces, as they were in a few, from about 1916 onwards, the Union would probably not have made any headway; conditions of service would have improved more rapidly and there would have been no strikes. But the confusion in the minds of the authorities between indiscipline and the making of complaints through authorised channels retarded the development of machinery for collective representations.

Not only was the strike of 1919 a failure, it also ruined the careers of the men who took part in it. They were all dismissed and none of them was ever reinstated. Many of them had been some of the best policemen, but the Government and police authorities felt that to reinstate any of the participants would look like condonation of the strike. The matter was thoroughly investigated by a Committee in 1924. The majority of the Committee recommended only some very small monetary compensation for the strikers, and legislation to this end was passed in 1926.

Miscellaneous Developments

When one considers that there were between 1829 and 1919 49 Acts of Parliament dealing with the organisation of the police or their conditions of service, it seems probable that many important matters have not been dealt with here, but there is no room to mention more than a few of these.

For many years the police of all ranks were subjected to political disabilities; but in 1887 it was thought safe to allow them to vote at parliamentary elections, and in 1893 at municipal elections.

The most important development of all was undoubtedly the provision in the Local Government Act, 1888, which gave the County Councils which it established some share in the administration of the police by substituting for the justices joint committees of county councillors and justices. More will be said about this measure in chapter V.

As the efficiency and numbers of the regular police increased during the 19th century, special constables were used less frequently, but they were in vogue again from about 1910 onwards, first in connection with industrial disturbances and then during the war of 1914–1918. Under the Act of 1831, the justices could only appoint special constables in effect at a time of crisis, but since 1914 there has been power to appoint and maintain a force of special constables in all police districts at all times. It is interesting to observe that under the Act of 1831 a man could be compelled to serve for a few months as a special constable unless he was in one of the exempt classes, and even the exempt could be ordered to serve by the Home Secretary if all those eligible had been appointed and more were required. The Home Secretary could also direct that special constables should be appointed throughout a county, and any person who refused to serve was liable to punishment. Clearly the direction of labour during the second world war was not as new a thing as some people thought. These parts of the Act of 1831 are incidentally still on the statute book, but have not been used for many years. It has at last been realised that it is no use compelling a man to be an unpaid policeman against his will.

CHAPTER III

Recent History:
1919-1949

Reforms

THE years 1900–1914 had been a stagnant period in the police. The war of 1914–1918 naturally woke the service up, but it also intensified some of its shortcomings. There were, as we have seen, difficulties due to poor and varying conditions of service and lack of representative machinery, and the system suffered severely from the fact that each of the 190 forces exercised almost complete autonomy on the operational side and often found it difficult to co-operate with others in the detection of offenders. Moreover, they had no common services, e.g. forensic science laboratories or central training schools; nor had they made adequate provision for assisting each other in times of crisis. Police authorities were indeed empowered by the Police Act, 1890, to enter into agreements as to the terms upon which members of one force might be lent to another in an emergency, but the system was cumbrous and these agreements did not bind one police authority to help another: each authority remained free to refuse or accede to requests for assistance.

The period 1919–1921 saw many reforms. The Police Federation was set up. The pay and conditions of service of the lower ranks in all forces were standardised and substantially improved, and the administration of discipline was made less arbitrary by the institution of a common discipline code. Consultative machinery in the form of the Police Council was instituted. In 1921 the law relating to police pensions was consolidated and some improvements in pensions introduced. Exchequer grant was increased so as to amount to half the cost of all expenditure on the police. The Home Secretary, having more powers, was able to put more pressure than previously on police authorities to make their forces efficient and more able to help each other.

There was thus from 1919 onwards increased centralisation in the administration of the police, but this was mainly concerned with pay and conditions of service. Little effort was made to secure more uniform action in the enforcement of the law, and the Government did not interfere more than it had done in the past with the executive actions of the police. This was, of course, a good thing, but the Home Secretary might with advantage have tried to secure more uniformity on the technical side of police work—e.g. standardised methods of recording crimes and criminals. It would, however, have been difficult for him to have done much in face of the unco-operative attitude of many police authorities and Chief Constables. Reforms on these matters were not made to any considerable extent until the late nineteen-thirties. For this delay there seems little justification: standardisation and centralisation on such matters do not endanger the personal liberty of the law-abiding citizen or infringe local autonomy on vital issues: they merely make it rather easier for the police to do their work of detecting and catching criminals.

It is not proposed in this book, which is concerned mainly with the development and administration of the police, to discuss police powers and procedure, important though the subject is; but no account of the police in the nineteen-twenties would be complete without a brief mention of the fact that more accusations than usual were at this period made against the police, especially the Metropolitan police. They were said to use 'third degree' methods; to be corrupt and unreliable in giving evidence; to interfere unnecessarily with the public, and in particular to be unduly severe on motorists and prostitutes. Many of these allegations were exaggerated, but that there were grounds for uneasiness was borne out by the most notable incidents of the period: the Savidge case of 1928, in which the action of the police in connection with their interrogation of Miss Savidge was criticised; and certain convictions for corruption, i.e. of Liverpool constables in 1927, and of Sergeant Goddard of the Metropolitan police in 1928. Public confidence was to some extent restored largely as a result of the investigations made by the Committee on certain Street Offences (1928) and by the Royal Com mission on Police Powers and Procedure (1929). The Committee on Street Offences which considered the practices of the police in connection with prostitution and solicitation came to the conclusion that the police did not make more mistakes in this type of case than in others, but they recommended that the police should take more care, especially when working in plain clothes. The Royal Commission, whose report is of permanent interest and value, reported that there was little support for the charge that the police generally were more arbitrary and oppressive in their attitude towards the public than they were before the war; on the contrary they formed a very favourable opinion of the conduct, tone, and efficiency of the police service as a whole. Nevertheless they made a number of important recommendations with a view to improving matters, and it is unfortunate that few of these were implemented. Relations between the police and the public, however, improved gradually, though there were difficulties during the nineteen-thirties also, mainly in connection with demonstrations by the unemployed and the activities of the British Union of Fascists.

Pay and Conditions of Service

When new scales of police pay were introduced in 1919, the settlement did not include any provision for the alteration of these scales in relation to any subsequent changes in the cost of living or in the general level of wages or anything else. The Desborough Committee had suggested that the new scales should be reviewed from time to time, but gave no indication of what change in circumstances would in their view warrant a change in pay. This was unfortunate and gave rise to many difficulties between the wars. For the Government usually considered that the real value of police pay should remain fairly constant, which in practice meant that it should fall with the fall in the cost of living; whereas to the police it seemed as if there was constant and unfair pressure to take away what they had gained in 1919 and no guarantee that pay would rise if the cost of living rose. In fact, during the only period when the cost of living rose, that is from 1919 to 1921, the Home Secretary increased the pay of the Metropolitan police and recommended all police authorities to do likewise, but there was no provision for automatic increases.

Nor was there any provision for automatic decreases, and in fact these were for the most part postponed by the Home Secretary until his hands were forced by an economic crisis. This happened twice: in 1922 and in 1931. In 1922, pay was reduced by $2\frac{1}{2}$ per cent., temporarily at first, but permanently from 1926 onwards when the reduction was turned into a contribution towards pensions. Rent allowances were also reduced for a time. Serious unrest resulted. On this occasion, however, there was machinery through which grievances could be legitimately voiced, and no strikes occurred as in 1918 and 1919. On the contrary the police were busily engaged in coping with industrial troubles culminating in the General Strike. The economy measures also involved a reduction in strengths. This was very unwelcome to H.M. Inspectors who had mostly been pressing police authorities to increase their forces. Many new duties, particularly traffic duties, were being put on the police at this time, and it was difficult for them to shoulder these with reduced numbers.

In spite of this reduction in pay, it seems that the real income of the police improved between 1926 and 1931, or, in other words, that their pay improved both in relation to average wages in other occupations, and to the amount of goods it would buy. Nevertheless, pay was not reduced again until 1931. Then both temporary and permanent cuts were made: reductions of 5 to 10 per cent. for all ranks until 1935, and lower rates for new entrants to the service (62s. a week rising in 12 years to 90s. as contrasted with 70s., rising in 10 years to 90s.). The reduction of the pay of new entrants received the approval of a committee—the Higgins Committee—which was set up in 1932 to make a thorough review of the subject. This committee naïvely believed that the reductions it recommended would be readily accepted by the police service, and that any disappointment which might then exist would quickly pass away. In this they were proved over optimistic. The reductions were at first strongly opposed by the Police Federation, and though they did not renew their opposition until 1939, from then onwards, until the Higgins scale was abolished in 1945, the Federation pressed for its abolition. They argued *inter alia* that it was introduced as a temporary economy measure and that the need for economy had passed. The Home Office, on the other hand, maintained that the alteration recommended by the Higgins Committee was independent of the financial crisis. There was some truth in both points of view: it is difficult to believe that the Higgins Committee was uninfluenced by the atmosphere of crisis in which they sat; but, on the other hand, the reduction they recommended was justifiable if the real value of the 1919 settlement was to remain unchanged.

Recent Increases in Pay

During the war of 1939–1945 the police were paid a war bonus partly to compensate them for extra work and responsibilities and partly as a result of a general tendency for all wages to rise. At the end of the war new scales giving some increase in pay were introduced. These did not satisfy the Police Federation, who maintained a steady pressure for higher scales. By the autumn of 1946 they had convinced the Home Secretary and police authorities that another increase was justified and this resulted in the introduction of new scales. The settlement then reached included not only an increase in pay, but improvements in other conditions of service. The Federation agreed that the new pay scales should remain unchanged until 1950 and the Home Secretary undertook to appoint an independent committee to review the whole field of police conditions of service and to report to him before the end of 1949. It was not long, however, before the Federation sought to reopen the bargain. They pressed strongly for an immediate increase in pay which neither the police authorities nor the Home Secretary felt justified in considering. In deference, however, to views strongly expressed in the Police Council and in Parliament, the Government decided that the review by an independent committee should be undertaken a year earlier than was originally intended. A committee under the chairmanship of Lord Oaksey was therefore set up.

The Police Federation asked for increases in pay ranging from 33½ to 54 per cent. for the ranks which they represented. By contrast the local authority associations, representing police authorities, recommended little or no increase. The Oaksey Committee came to the conclusion that the police were underpaid and recommended increases ranging between 10 and 20 per cent. for all ranks. The following considerations appear to have been responsible for this recommendation. (1) The rate of resignations from the police, especially young men in the middle years of service, was disturbingly high, and though pay was not the only, it was an important, factor in attracting recruits and retaining serving men. (2) Police duties and responsibilities were more exacting than in 1919, but pay had not increased proportionately. The police should be treated more like members of the professional classes than as unskilled workers. (3) Increases in police pay granted since 1939 had fallen short of the improvements made in other occupations, especially when hours of work and night and week-end duty were taken into account. (4) It was essential that members of police forces should be contented and reasonably free from financial worry.

Let us examine these arguments one by one.

(1) It is difficult to determine what factors affect recruitment and prevent wastage, and how high pay has to be to have an appreciable effect on them, but one of the obvious ways of trying to induce men to join and stay in the police is to improve their pay and conditions of service. The fact that only a small number of men and women have the requisite qualities of mind and body to undertake police work may mean that we must pay them more (not less, as seems curiously enough to be suggested by the Oaksey Committee) to attract and retain them than if the supply were greater.

(2) Before 1919, a policeman in the lowest rank was paid at, broadly speaking, the same rate as an agricultural or unskilled labourer, though the policeman had various extra emoluments such as pension rights which brought his total real income above that of the labourer. The Desborough Committee made out a strong case for paying the police more than unskilled labourers and the new rates adopted in 1919 gave effect to this view. By 1949 it appeared that police duties had increased in number and complexity since 1919: the police had, for instance, to deal with better-equipped criminals, a whole new range of offences and people drawn from a wider range of society than before. There is something in this argument, but it should not be used without considering whether the responsibilities and duties of workers in other occupations have not also increased. If they have, there is no ground for increasing police pay alone, and no point in increasing everyone's pay.

(3) The passages in the Oaksey Committee's report dealing with changes since 1939 in police and other workers' pay are not as full and as documented with statistics as one would wish. It is admittedly difficult to compare police remuneration with rates of wages in other occupations because of (a) the 'concealed' or extra emoluments the police receive, the value of some of which is not agreed, and (b) differences in hours of work and overtime arrangements, and payment by piece rates in some occupations. Nevertheless, the following table may be of some value.

Percentage increases in rates of pay since 1938

		Oaksey rates
Police, excluding extra emoluments	1948	1949
Constable on his minimum . .	69	105
Constable on his maximum . .	47	69
Sergeant on his minimum . . .	50	71
Sergeant on his maximum . . .	46	65
Other occupations	October, 1948	April, 1949
Adult male manual workers in manufacturing and principal non-manufacturing industries, excluding overtime	60	62

If increases in the value of the extra emoluments of the police and the amount earned by working overtime in the case of the other occupations were included, the figures above would probably all rise about proportionately.

It would seem, therefore, that the Oaksey Committee's rates of pay for the police improve their position relative to other workers, but there is perhaps some justification for this in view of the disabilities which attach to police service, such as the liability of policemen to be called for duty at any time and the rule which forbids them supplementing their wages by doing other work in their spare time.

(4) The last argument used by the Oaksey Committee—that it is essential that policemen should be reasonably contented and free from financial worry—does not really help very much in fixing rates of pay and can be pushed too far. For there might come a point where we should prefer to do without most of our police rather than pay them what they needed to make them even reasonably contented. On the other hand, if the Oaksey Committee is saying no more than that it is very important, if not essential, to ensure that the employees in certain vital services such as the police (and there are many others) are not so discontented that they will strike, the proposition can be accepted.

The first part of the Oaksey Committee's report was issued in the spring of 1949 and discussed at a Police Council meeting. The local authorities represented on the Council accepted the committee's proposals, which seems strange in the light of the views they had expressed to the committee; and the Government implemented the committee's recommendations without delay. Pay was fixed at the following weekly rates: for constables £6 7s. rising to £8 1s., and for sergeants £8 11s. rising to £9 6s. 8d. If to the basic pay of the police at the above rates are added their other emoluments, that is, the value of free quarters or a rent allowance, uniform and the value of their pensions, the figures above would, on a reasonable estimate, be roughly as follows: constables £9 6s. to £11 8s., and sergeants £12 3s. to £13 5s.

The average actual weekly earnings of adult male manual workers, skilled and unskilled, in manufacturing and the principal non-manufacturing industries in April, 1949, were £7 with no extra emoluments. It will be seen, therefore, that the policeman, even when he starts as a young man, is much better remunerated than the average manual worker. This is no doubt justifiable, but the total cost of the increases—£4 million a year apart from the effect on future pensions—is very high. Police pay, before the increases, cost £25 to £26 million annually, so that even when considered as a proportion of the previous cost, the increases are by no means negligible.

It may have been essential if wastage was to be diminished to have increased pay in 1949 as much as was done, but the police were undoubtedly lucky. There is only one paragraph in the Oaksey Committee's report in which the question is considered in the light of the White Paper of 1948 on Personal Incomes, Costs and Prices, and the report contains little detailed comparison of police pay with wages in other occupations in which conditions of service and responsibilities are similar enough to make a comparison useful. Moreover, the police got their improved pay only two months before the economic crisis of September, 1949. If the matter had not been settled by then, they would probably have fared much less well.

The police were also fortunate in that increased pay was not coupled with any alteration, except a minor one, in the scale of their pensions. Police retirement pensions are very generous and their cost (about £10 million a year) is very high and still rising. About one-fifth of the cost is borne by the police themselves by means of contributions, and the remainder by public funds. The Oaksey Committee did not, unfortunately, think that it was for them to review police pensions thoroughly, but reported that if they had, they would have recommended less generous benefits. The Government, when agreeing to increased pay, did not at the same time announce that it proposed to undertake a thorough review of police pensions and it now seems improbable that this will be done. The Committee optimistically remarked that it seemed likely that a review would become necessary (meaning apparently would be undertaken) in the future; but the time to have done this would have been when pay was increased: it is more difficult to do it later. One long-overdue minor reform in the pension arrangements which was adverse to the police was made, but that was all.

The only way to mitigate the burden of police expenditure is to try to do with less policemen. It should be the aim of all police authorities to cut down the number of police they employ without lowering the standard of execution of essential police duties. This may be done by increased mechanisation, by the elimination of unnecessary work, the substitution of female typists and clerks for policemen in offices, and the replacement of policemen on specialist work, e.g. photography and finger-print identification, by non-police staff who need not be given the opportunity to retire at a comparatively early age on a large police pension.

The Failure to Amalgamate between the Wars

Just as reductions in pay put a brake between the wars on improvements in morale, so the continued existence of the smaller forces put a brake on improvements in efficiency. These forces maintained their independence in spite of recommendations to the contrary. Thus the Desborough Committee recommended the abolition of all police forces in non-county boroughs in England and Wales and declared that ideally a town with a population of less than 100,000 should not have a separate force. It also recommended that no new force should be established in a county borough except with the consent of the Home Secretary and that consent should not be given unless some definite administrative advantage would result. The non-county boroughs immediately organised strong opposition to these proposals. They were not embodied in the Police Act, 1919, but a clause was inserted in the Economy (Miscellaneous Provisions) Bill of 1922 giving the Home Secretary power to impose mergers on police authorities in certain circumstances. The Government hoped to save about £20,000 by these mergers, though they admitted that this estimate was highly conjectural; but the bill was severely criticised mainly for its other clauses and withdrawn. The Government intended to introduce separate Bills to cover the same ground, but did not do so in the case of the police.

The Royal Commission on Local Government which was appointed in 1923 took a good deal of evidence about the optimum size of police areas, but did not make any recommendation on the matter as it considered that it was for the Government to decide what to do in the light of the Desborough report. The Home Office witness, giving his personal view, said the existence of so many separate forces was an absurdity and certainly a source of weakness and inefficiency from the police point of view. If the matter could be considered as *res integra*, a reasonable unit of administration for police purposes would in his view be a quarter of a million persons for county and borough forces alike, that is, on the standards then prevailing, forces of about 250 men in counties and 300 men in boroughs. This would have involved the abolition of at least half the forces in the country. Such a radical suggestion does not seem to have been made again until changes of this order were recommended by the Local Government Boundary Commission in 1947.

When suitable opportunities occurred the Home Secretary and Inspectors put a little mild pressure on police authorities to amalgamate, but apparently no Home Secretary threatened to withhold the Exchequer grant between the wars in order to bring about amalgamations. It was probably considered that it would not be right to try to secure changes of this kind by administrative action and that they should be specifically sanctioned by Parliament. Moreover, there were legal obstacles in the way of amalgamations other than amalgamations of boroughs with counties. The result was that very few amalgamations took place: between 1920 and 1939 only eight borough forces merged themselves with the surrounding county, and four of these mergers took place in 1921.

A select committee of the House of Commons was set up in 1932 as a result, it would seem, of the economy campaign of that year. The committee pointed out that the size of forces and the populations they served varied greatly, there being then 14 forces with 25 men or less serving populations of less than 20,000, the minimum population which was thought by Parliament suitable for a police area in 1877; but this committee's recommendations were much more moderate than the Desborough Committee's. Rejecting the suggestion of the Home Office that the limit should be a population of 75,000, it suggested the much lower minimum of 30,000. Even this would have involved the merging of 28 forces. The committee also expressed the pious hope that voluntary amalgamations between county and county borough forces would take place.

Between 1932 and 1939 the Government was constantly pressed to implement the committee's report, but it did not do so, whether because of shortage of parliamentary time or fear of touching a prickly subject, it is not clear. Meanwhile the Inspectors reported that some forces were too small to provide for themselves the simplest equipment, and the Departmental Committee on Detective work and Procedure, which from 1933 to 1938 made a thorough enquiry into the organisation and procedure of police forces, laid special emphasis on the advantages of amalgamating small forces. But it needed a second world war to embolden a Government to take action which had been recommended on and off for many years by many different bodies.

The Second World War

(i) *Preparations and Man Power*

Unlike the fire service, the police service survived the war of 1939–1945 without being nationalised. Nor was it regionalised. Certain changes, of course, took place: the Defence Regulations gave the Home Secretary wide powers of control over all forces; the police had to fit themselves into the Civil Defence regional organisation; 21 out of the 183 forces which existed in 1939 were amalgamated during the war with other forces; and the Exchequer bore the whole cost of certain, not unimportant, items of expenditure. But the salient features of the organisation of the police service remained unchanged: there were in 1945 still 159 separate, independent forces, all except one maintained by local police authorities.

The year 1939 was a severe testing time for the police. The Home Office could not simply order local police authorities to prepare for ' an emergency'—the euphemistic term for 'war' which is used in peace-time. Therefore, however likely the Government thought a war, it could not, whilst maintaining the essential features of a locally run police service, ensure that all the preparations which it thought necessary were made. The result was that some forces were far better prepared than others. Differences in forces which already existed in peace-time were emphasised when there was a sudden demand for expansion and added responsibilities had to be shouldered. Some police authorities did not believe there would be a war; others, whatever they thought about the probability of war, were mainly concerned with avoiding extra expenditure. This attitude is understandable, but it naturally caused acute concern to H.M. Inspectors and to those Chief Constables whose proposals were not approved by their police authorities. This is the price paid for local control of a service.

Nevertheless, in most forces preparations were made: strengths were increased, auxiliaries were recruited and trained, communications were improved, and Air Raid Precautions and anti-gas training was given. Plans for fitting in to the Civil Defence Services were worked out and the ordinary arrangements for mutual aid between the forces were improved. In order to encourage police authorities to build up adequate reserves of auxiliaries, the Government announced it would bear the whole cost of the pay of the bulk of the auxiliaries, that is, of the Police War Reserve, full-time Special Constables, and the Women's Auxiliary Police Corps. Encouraged by this step, some local authorities argued that the Government should be responsible for all expenditure connected with the war, or, as they sometimes put it, for measures which were necessary in the national and not only in the local interest. The distinction would have been difficult to draw in practice, and in any event the Government would not accept the principle.

At first these auxiliaries, or temporary constables as they were sometimes called, were employed wholly on war duties, e.g. Air Raid Precautions, guarding vulnerable points, etc., but as time went on and more and more of the regular police were released to the armed forces, the auxiliaries were used increasingly for ordinary police duty until by the end of the war they were largely interchangeable with the regular police. The Government, nevertheless, bore their whole cost until halfway through 1945; after that date half the cost fell on the rates. For two or three years these temporary constables constituted as much as about a third of the total strength of the police.

Volunteers were at first available in sufficient numbers, but, as local sources of recruitment dried up, action by the central authority became necessary to maintain establishments. Not only were temporary constables, like the permanent police, 'frozen', that is, forbidden to leave their employment without permission, but power was taken under the National Service Act, 1941, to call up men for service in the Police War Reserve as an alternative to service in the armed forces. These conscripts were allocated by the Home Office to the forces which most needed recruits, and were transferred from force to force and discharged from the police service by the Home Secretary. The system was a new departure, for normally police officers are volunteers and are recruited by each Chief Constable or Watch Committee, but, though there were difficulties, the experiment proved more successful than was expected.

These measures—the payment by the Government of the whole cost of the auxiliaries and the posting of conscripts to the individual forces—could be regarded as instances of war-time encroachment by the central authority into the sphere of local police authorities, but they did not entail any interference by the Government in the executive functions of the police. The Government admittedly determined the pay and conditions of service of the auxiliaries without consultation with police authorities—they were in fact fixed in relation to those of Civil Defence workers—but they did not give orders to individual auxiliaries; and whilst there were inevitably during the war tendencies towards centralisation, these are not instances of them. The auxiliaries were not a national police force at the beck and call of the Government.

(ii) *Regional Organisation*

On the outbreak of war, England and Wales were divided for Civil Defence purposes into 11 regions each one of which was in charge of a Regional Commissioner. The duties of these Commissioners were to co-ordinate the Civil Defence plans and activities of Government Departments and local authorities, and in the case of a breakdown in communications to act for the central Government. They were also responsible for the operational control of the Civil Defence Services during air raids, and had certain administrative duties delegated to them.

Close co-operation between the police and the Civil Defence Services was secured at the local level by the fact that the police played a prominent part in organising and developing the Air Raid

Precautions Services. In many cases the Chief Constable was also the Civil Defence Controller, and the police were responsible for the organisation and supervision of the wardens' service. It was also necessary to fit the police into the regional machinery. This was not always easy. Police authorities and Chief Constables retained their responsibilities and powers and had to perform their normal functions, considerably widened by war conditions, under the direct authority of the Home Office; but they had at the same time to dovetail into the inevitably intricate Civil Defence machinery, with its regional organisation and its local emergency committees. Liaison between the police and the regional organisation was provided by the appointment to each regional headquarters (except London) of certain officers known as Acting Inspectors of Constabulary and police staff officers. Their duties were to keep Regional Commissioners informed of police matters and Chief Constables informed of regional schemes in so far as they affected the police. They were also to assist the Inspectors of Constabulary on matters relating to the war. As the war went on, the work of these police staffs at regions increased in importance: they assisted with Civil Defence and military exercises, helped to plan schemes for police reinforcements in each region, and co-ordinated police plans for troop movements and convoys. They were also the focal point to which information was sent by the police forces and from which consolidated information was passed to the Home Office.

Even if the Civil Defence Regions had not been set up, it seems probable that the need for some police regional machinery would have been felt at any rate by the military, if not by the Home Office. There might well have been more amalgamations of forces if it had not been for the police regional organisation, and realisation of this in police circles may have accounted for a certain abatement of hostility to all things regional.

It is not, however, true that this police regional machinery was a great experiment in regional government. Regional Commissioners gave, admittedly, operational orders to Chief Constables during air raids, in matters connected with Civil Defence. The most usual form this took was to direct a Chief Constable to send assistance to a neighbouring force. But nothing like the regionalisation of the police service took place, for police authorities and Chief Constables were not subordinated to Regional Commissioners except on operational matters in air raids. In so far as there was a shift of power in police matters during the war, it was much more to the Home Secretary than to Regions, though there was continual pressure by Regional Commissioners to get control of the police. But the regional machinery accustomed Chief Constables to work together in regions rather more than they had previously, though even this was starting before the war with certain services which were organised on a regional basis. Further changes in this direction have taken place since the war, but these may more properly be regarded as the descendants of the pre-war development than of the Civil Defence regional organisation.

(iii) *Amalgamations*

In spite of the regional machinery, it was thought necessary to amalgamate a number of forces with each other in certain districts. The Defence (Amalgamation of Police Forces) Regulations, 1942, empowered the Home Secretary to make an order amalgamating two or more forces in any area in which he was satisfied this was necessary for facilitating naval, military or air force operations. In defending the regulations in the House of Commons, the Home Secretary said that he had no intention of establishing a national police force, or even regional police forces. All he wanted to do was to merge two small forces into one, or a small force into a bigger one, in certain areas, in order to assist the armed forces who often found it difficult with so many small police forces to know with which one they should deal. A simpler organisation of the police service would help them and would ensure rather more uniformity of policy in strategically important areas. The Home Secretary thought the regulations might well have been made earlier; the coming of the American armies had tipped the balance and had decided him to take power to amalgamate forces in areas which were liable to invasion or which were important in relation to offensive military operations.

In 1943 the Home Secretary made orders under the regulations reducing by 21 the number of forces in the south of England. The regulations and the orders made under them met at first with much opposition especially from the borough police authorities which were to be merged. The Home Secretary was suspected of sinister intentions; local authorities feared that there would not be a return

E 2

to the pre-war position when the regulations lapsed; displaced Chief Constables did not like being told they could retire or be demoted to superintendents, although the financial terms for those retiring were not ungenerous. But most of these difficulties were gradually overcome. The ordinary policeman found that he was not affected, except in some cases by an improvement in conditions, as all had to be raised to the level of the highest; and it was felt in most quarters that in so far as there had been a change, it was a change for the better.

One rather curious outcome of these war-time amalgamations was the extension of a policeman's right of appeal to the Home Secretary in disciplinary cases. The disciplinary arrangements in borough forces are, as we have seen, different from those in county forces. The result was that a borough police officer whose force was amalgamated with a county force in effect lost a right of appeal to the police authority from the decision of the Chief Constable. The solution devised was to give to all police officers an extended right of appeal to the Home Secretary against the decision of the disciplinary authority (whether Chief Constable or police authority): as the law then stood, they could only appeal where the punishment was dismissal or enforced resignation; in future they could appeal against a reduction in rank or rate of pay.

(iv) Control of Police Forces under the Defence Regulations

While it is true that the police service survived the war with its structure unscathed—except for the amalgamations—the Government not unnaturally decided that it could not run any risks. In peace time it might not matter vitally if the 183 police forces all pursued different policies, but in war-time there might well be matters on which uniformity was essential and the local police authorities might not succumb to gentle persuasion. There might also be a weak force which was not only a danger to itself but to its neighbours. The Government therefore armed itself with powers of a most comprehensive character.

By Defence Regulation 39 of the Defence (General) Regulations, the Home Secretary could give to any police authority or Chief Officer of police such general or special instructions as appeared to him necessary or expedient in the interests of the public safety, the defence of the realm, the maintenance of public order or the efficient prosecution of the war. Such instructions had effect not-withstanding any restriction or limitation imposed by or under any Act. The Regulation also specifically provided that the Home Secretary could require a Chief Officer of police to retire if he did not consider him fit to perform his duties in the conditions which prevailed or might be expected to prevail in his area. Very few formal instructions were given by the Home Secretary under this Defence Regulation, but he threatened to use his powers on a number of occasions, particularly to secure the retirement of Chief Constables who could not stand up to the strain of the war, and it was undoubtedly most useful for him to possess them.

As in many other spheres, so in that of the police the war pro-vided a curious stimulus to reform. It was obvious that in some things, such as recruitment and training, the war had created certain problems to which a solution would have to be found as peace drew nearer; but there were many other things—from police boxes to a police college—which were at this time examined afresh, not because the war had made this necessary, but because it led people to question things which they had accepted passively in peace-time. When violent changes, both physical and social, take place as they did in the last war, it is difficult to think of any institutions or customs as immutable, and even those who are usually the most stalwart upholders of the *status quo* are to be found considering the possibility of change.

So it came about that in 1944 the Home Secretary and Secretary of State for Scotland appointed a committee consisting of repre-sentatives of their Departments, Inspectors of Constabulary, and Chief Constables to consider not only immediate post-war prob-lems, but many questions of long-term policy. The most important of these was the establishment of a Police College for the training of the higher ranks. Other matters examined by the Committee included police buildings, prosecutions, policewomen, and the beat system. Little seems to have come of some of the reports, but the Post-War Committee, nevertheless, did some useful work and provided machinery, though imperfect, for the exploration of various problems and for the dissemination in police circles of new ideas.

The Police Act, 1946, and Post-war Amalgamations

When the war came to an end, it was necessary to decide what to do with the forces which had been amalgamated under the Defence Regulations. There were three possible courses. One was simply to let the regulations lapse and to revert to the pre-war, or rather pre-1943, position. This would have involved a good deal of laborious 'unscrambling'. Another possible course was to pass an Act of Parliament perpetuating in peace-time the war-time mergers, but not to add to them. The objection to this was that the 21 forces merged during the war were not the 21 forces one would have chosen to merge in peace-time. A third possible course was to take the opportunity to survey the whole police service in the light of the ideal size for a force, and to implement the recommendations which had been made on so many occasions in the past by committee after committee and Inspector after Inspector that the smaller forces should be abolished. The Home Secretary chose this course. A glance at the facts and figures will show that the strange thing is not that the Government decided in 1946 to rationalise to some extent the police service, but that the haphazard organisation of the past survived so long. For in 1945 there were in England and Wales 309 non-county boroughs. Forty-seven of these 309 had their own police force, but these were by no means the 47 largest or most important non-county boroughs. Of the remaining 262, 228 were policed by the surrounding county force, and 34, being in the Metropolitan police district, by the Metropolitan force. Of the 47 with their own forces, 14 had been merged with other forces under the Defence Regulations. There were also 72 county borough forces. Eight county boroughs did not have their own force and were policed by the surrounding county. There were also three county boroughs policed by the Metropolitan force. The size of the borough forces varied from 2,000 to 15; the size of the county forces from 2,500 to 10. With only three exceptions, each of the administrative counties (but not each of the geographical counties) had its force, however small.

Not only was the structure haphazard and unsymmetrical, but as the law then stood changes were unlikely to occur, and some combinations could not legally be made. A borough force (whether county or non-county) could merge itself in a county force if both parties agreed, but a county force could not amalgamate with another county force, nor a borough force with a borough force. Nor was there any provision for the establishment of joint police authorities: merging involved the abolition of the smaller force, not the establishment of a joint force. Various devices were used to do away with some of the absurdities: for instance, some neighbouring police authorities appointed the same Chief Constable, who was responsible for two (and in one instance three) forces, but who had to report to different police authorities—a most inconvenient arrangement.

It is not to be wondered at, therefore, that in 1945 the Home Secretary introduced a Bill into Parliament to do three things: to abolish non-county borough forces (with two exceptions); to permit amalgamations between two county forces or two borough forces; and to give himself powers to initiate compulsory amalgamation schemes subject to certain specified safeguards. In support of the Bill, the Home Secretary said that in the light of the facilities which were available to the modern criminal, there was an ever-increasing need for specialisation amongst police officers. The smaller forces could not maintain the necessary specialised departments and equipment. Promotion for efficient policemen should be better in a bigger force, and the larger forces should be more economical in overheads and man-power than the smaller. The Home Secretary said he thought a police force might be too big as well as too small; he did not intend to create regional police forces elsewhere of the size or type of the Metropolitan force, though he was not proposing to interfere with the size of the latter. He wished to retain the local character of the police; he appreciated the value of local knowledge and local tradition; but the maintenance of order and the prevention and detection of crime throughout the country were matters of national importance. There must therefore be a proper balance between civic pride and the claims of efficiency.

The Bill was hotly criticised both inside and outside Parliament. Many of the forces which it abolished belonged to small boroughs of antiquity and intense local pride, and it was not always easy for the people on the spot to perceive that modern police problems required the existence of police units which were large enough to provide the necessary specialist facilities. The provision for compulsory amalgamations by order of the Home Secretary was regarded as equally if not more iniquitous. It was suggested that he might use this power to nationalise the police: he might combine more and more forces together until there was only one left. The provision for a local enquiry before a compulsory order was made against the police authorities' wishes was said to be valueless: the person holding the enquiry would know the Home Secretary had made up his mind beforehand, and in any event his advice need not be taken. Ultimately the Home Secretary accepted an amendment that no county or county borough with a population of 100,000 or over should be compulsorily combined with an authority larger than itself, and the Bill was passed into law. Some people did not think this went far enough and wanted to limit the compulsory powers to areas with less than 60,000 inhabitants, but this would, in the Home Secretary's view, have wrecked the Bill. The Act also provided that the report of any enquiry was to be laid before Parliament.

Action under the Police Act, 1946, has until 1949 been as follows. On 1st April, 1947, 45 non-county borough police forces were abolished; the Watch Committees concerned lost all their police powers to the county police authority, and the area previously policed by the borough police was from thenceforth policed by the force of the surrounding county. Four voluntary amalgamation schemes have been made and approved by the Home Secretary. These combine the forces in the following areas: the Scilly Isles and Cornwall; Kent and Canterbury; Durham, West Hartlepool and Darlington (already partly consolidated); and the City and Liberty of Peterborough. In one case the opposite process took place: the county borough of Bournemouth which had never had a force of its own was allowed to have one. In view of the size of the town and of the undertakings given by the Home Secretary during the debates on the Police Act, no other decision was to be expected, though it runs counter to the general tendency in police administration to-day. Two compulsory orders have been made: one in 1947 to combine the forces of Breconshire, Montgomeryshire, and Radnorshire, and the other in 1949 to combine the forces of Chester and Cheshire. In the Welsh case, amalgamation, though initiated by the Home Secretary, first met with the approval of the county councils concerned, but they could not agree on the constitution of the joint authority. A compulsory order was therefore made by the Home Secretary after a public enquiry had been held and amalgamation had been recommended. An enquiry was also held in the

Cheshire case and resulted in an emphatic recommendation for amalgamation.

It is important to realise that the Police Act, 1946, distinguishes between abolition and amalgamation. The police authorities of the non-county boroughs were abolished and do not elect representatives to send to the county police authorities which took over their forces. But where amalgamation schemes are formed, whether voluntarily or compulsorily, the police authorities form a combined police authority and the constituent authorities each appoint a prescribed number of their members to serve on the combined police authority for a prescribed period.

Most of the combined police authorities so far set up under the Police Act, 1946, are responsible for areas which are not administered as units except for police purposes. It has long been recognised that different services can from the technical or administrative point of view often be best organised over different areas, and the device of setting up a separate body for each service to operate over the appropriate area has often been used. It was much in vogue in the 18th and 19th centuries. One of the best examples of such a body is the Commissioners of Police of the Metropolis who were in 1829 given control of the police over an area which was not a unit for any other governmental or administrative purpose. In recent years the device has again become common, but the trend of opinion is on the whole against organising services in this way and in favour of bringing as many services as possible within the scope of a compendious authority. This is not the place to review the arguments on either side, but to draw attention to the fact that the new combined police authorities are mostly responsible for *ad hoc* areas.

Writers about joint local authorities often divide them into joint boards and joint committees. The term 'joint board' is usually applied to executive bodies with precepting powers, and the term 'joint committee' is used for more informal bodies set up by agreement between two or more local authorities. On these definitions, combined police authorities are joint boards. The terms themselves are not important, but the analysis is useful as it focuses attention upon the powers of the joint authorities under examination. Thus a combined police authority constituted under the Police Act, 1946, is a body corporate, with a common seal and with power to hold land without licence in mortmain. It can sue or be sued; it can raise loans itself or through the constituent authorities; it can issue precepts on the constituent authorities; and its existence cannot be terminated by the constituent authorities.

It is too soon to say whether combined police authorities exemplify the weaknesses which are commonly said to attach to joint authorities, those, for instance, which are referred to in the report of the Local Government Boundary Commission for 1947. As the members of the combined police authorities so far set up are members of the constituent bodies, i.e. Standing Joint Committees, county borough councils, and Watch Committees, there seems no ground for saying that combined police authorities are not directly financially responsible. It is true that the county and borough councils concerned have to pay to the combined police authority their share, calculated as laid down in the statutory order, of the expenses of the combined police authority, but they can presumably question their representatives on the combined authority about its policy and expenditure and can instruct them as to the policy they are to advocate. Indeed in some respects the combined authority could be said to have more direct financial responsibility than a Watch Committee has in an uncombined area, as there the borough council is the authority with ultimate financial responsibility. Incidentally, one of the arguments for amalgamation has been that it would result in economies. It is too soon to say whether this has been the effect up to now, and it would be helpful if sometime a thorough enquiry into the financial results of amalgamation were conducted.

Another alleged weakness of joint authorities is a tendency on the part of the members to regard themselves as representatives and advocates of their own councils rather than as members of a common body. This may well be a danger, but at the same time it helps to preserve as close contact as possible between the members of the joint authority and the area which they represent. Unless this is done, the disadvantages of indirect election will manifest themselves. Of course, much depends on the wise selection of the members of the joint authority. If membership is awarded rather as a reward for long service than on grounds of fitness for the work, obviously the joint authority will suffer. But if the members chosen are the best from each of the constituent authorities, the joint authority should be stronger than any of its makers.

In conclusion, what judgment are we to pass on the Police Act, 1946, and on the orders made under it? From the technical and administrative point of view, the changes made are almost certainly an improvement. It is admittedly difficult to find a scientific yardstick with which to compare police efficiency before and after amalgamation, but those who are in a position to form a judgment of value based on wide experience of police work consider that the changes were desirable and have strengthened the police service. On the other hand, the changes are regretted by most members of police authorities who lost their forces and by some members of authorities where a combined force has been formed. After the initial shock, they were probably little regretted by the members of the forces. But we must not look at these changes only from the technical and administrative point of view; we must not only consider whether there have been created 'effective and convenient units of local government administration', to use the language of the instruction to the Local Government Boundary Commission; we must see whether these developments infringe certain principles which most democrats and believers in local government think important.

Mr. C. H. Wilson, in his recent essay on the 'Foundations of Local Government' (Blackwell, 1948), suggests that local government is valuable because it enables many people to participate in governing, and because it provides political education. He writes: 'If men are clear that what they hope to get out of local government is not only sweeter drains, roomier houses, greener parks, but an exercise of their own adult civic responsibility and political education, then the foundation of local government is sound, and soundly understood.'

Mr. Wilson also stresses the importance of government being intelligible to the citizens of a state. On the whole, the abolition and amalgamation of police authorities result in fewer people participating in local government, discussing the issues, acquiring political education. As to intelligibility, the balance is probably about even: a system under which a borough and a county force have their headquarters in the same town, but function apparently independently of each other, is not intelligible to most people. On the other hand, amalgamation may be said to diminish intelligibility by giving opportunities to fewer persons to get to know their police force by managing it.

This supplies a healthy antidote to the technical approach, but leaves us to settle what should be done when the ideals of 'efficiency' and 'political education' conflict, as of course they may. We should not be misled into maintaining tens of thousands of expensive policemen in order to give ourselves opportunities to exercise civic responsibility and to educate ourselves politically. In considering how to organise our police forces, our chief objective should be to enable them to fulfil police functions more efficiently; if incidentally we can learn to exercise civic responsibility and to understand the society in which we live, this will be to the good.

The Police Act, 1946, may have seemed radical to some people, but the Local Government Boundary Commission in its report for 1947 made even more radical proposals. Of the three main types of local authority recommended by the Commission, only two, namely the one-tier and the two-tier counties, would have responsibility for the police. This would mean that there would be independent police forces only in towns with populations of more than 200,000 inhabitants and, with some exceptions, in the present administrative counties. The number of police forces would be reduced from 129 to about 70. Probably a few more amalgamations will take place during the next few years—one or two others are already being discussed*; but as the recommendations of the Boundary Commission are, on present plans, not to be implemented, it appears unlikely that there will be any substantial changes in the structure of police authorities and areas.

* At the time of going to press, the three counties of Anglesey, Carnarvon and Merioneth had agreed to combine from 1st October, 1950; and the Home Secretary had proposed the amalgamation of: (a) Cardiganshire, Pembrokeshire and Carmarthenshire; (b) the boroughs of Dewsbury and Wakefield with the West Riding of Yorkshire; and (c) Leicestershire and Rutland. The Home Secretary's proposals are said to have met with opposition.

CHAPTER IV

Central Control

'THE police is not a local service. Every force in the country is controlled from beginning to end by the Home Office. It is a local service in that we are permitted to pay half the cost of it. Members of Watch Committees imagine themselves to be very important people, but can do nothing.' Thus spake a member of a Watch Committee in 1946. Only a few years before then a Home Secretary said he exercised only a 'curious kind of supervisory power' over provincial police authorities. He could not send a single policeman from a provincial force to a disturbance without the consent of the police authority; and he could not have anyone arrested at his whim whether with the consent of the authority or not. Where such different views are held, it may be difficult to lay clear the truth. The best thing will be as a start to examine the forms of control, apart from the Home Secretary's powers to amalgamate two or more forces which have already been discussed.

The Home Secretary's Regulations

Under the Police Act, 1919, the Home Secretary may make regulations as to the government, mutual aid, pay, allowances, clothing, expenses and conditions of service of the members of all police forces in England and Wales, and every police authority is to comply with the regulations so made. These regulations do not have to be laid before Parliament, but they must be submitted in draft to the Police Council, and any representations made by the Council must be considered by the Home Secretary before he makes the regulations.

Regulations known as 'The Police Regulations' (not to be confused with regulations made by the police to control, e.g. traffic) were made under the Police Act in 1920. They prescribed a wide range of conditions of service. Their main framework is still the same to-day, though some new provisions have been introduced and some of the original ones have been altered or revoked. The regulations, which were last consolidated in 1948, are published as Statutory Rules and Orders. There is a separate though very similar code for policewomen. The following matters are prescribed in the regulations: names of ranks, qualifications for appointment, disciplinary procedure, rules for promotion, hours of duty, annual leave, scales of pay for the lower ranks, some allowances, and issues of clothing. The regulations also require that various matters which are settled in the first place by the police authority shall be subject to the Home Secretary's approval. These include the size of the force and the numbers in each rank, appointments to the post of Chief Constable, scales of pay for the higher ranks, rent allowances and other allowances not prescribed in the regulations.

Mutual aid, i.e. the giving of aid by one force to another, is not dealt with in the Police Regulations, although it is amongst the matters which the Home Secretary has power to regulate under the Act of 1919. Arrangements for mutual aid have been made from time to time by groups of forces, often after stimulation by the Home Office. Between the wars H.M. Inspectors often commented on the inadequacy of these arrangements. The Home Office issued model terms and conditions upon which assistance should be given, but no force was under any obligation to help another and it is difficult to see why such an obligation was not imposed by a regulation. Since the second world war the Home Secretary has had power under the Defence Regulations to instruct a police authority or Chief Officer to assist another force where this appeared necessary or expedient in the interests of the public safety or the maintenance of public order, but these powers have not been used and it seems unlikely that they will be: the voluntary mutual aid agreements between forces are regarded as adequate.

The Home Secretary also has power to make regulations regarding police pensions. These regulations are made under the Police Pensions Act, 1948, and not under the Police Act, 1919. Before 1948 police pensions were governed by statutes, but the tendency recently has been to favour prescribing the details in regulations which will make it easier to rectify any anomalies which come to light. Before making such regulations, the Home Secretary must consult the Police Council, and the Regulations are subject to the consent of the Treasury and to affirmative resolution by Parliament.

The Police Pensions Regulations made in 1948 form an elaborate pensions code.

It will be seen, therefore, that the Home Secretary's Regulations lay down a comprehensive code dealing with the main conditions of service of all police officers. Few people with any experience of the administration of the police question the necessity of this, though they may think the regulations prescribe conditions in too much detail. The matters which are actually laid down in the regulations, e.g. scales of pay for the lowest ranks, and hours of duty, seldom lead to difficulties with police authorities, whose representatives have been consulted when they were being framed. There may be an occasional case where two views are taken as to the meaning of the regulation, or where through inadvertence it has not been complied with. Such cases are normally taken up by the man affected or by the Police Federation on his behalf with the Chief Constable or police authority. If the matter gets as far as the Home Office, the Home Secretary will enquire into it and inform the Chief Constable or the police authority of his views and ask them to put the matter right.

Difficulties between police authorities and the Home Secretary do, however, sometimes arise in connection with the matters which are settled in the first place locally, but are subject to the Home Secretary's approval. The most controversial of these are the strength of forces and the appointment of Chief Constables.

Before 1920, the Home Office did not closely supervise the strength of the various forces. It confined itself to seeing that the numbers were reasonably sufficient for minimum requirements and not excessively extravagant. Police authorities had a wide discretion, and, even allowing for different local conditions, the standard of policing was much more generous in some areas than others. In 1922 the Geddes Committee recommended that a formula based on various facts—the acreage, population and rateable value of the area—should be used to calculate the number of police required in each district, and the Exchequer grant limited accordingly. The Home Office considered that this would have carried central supervision too far and that to determine the strength of the several forces on a hard and fast rule without reference to special local conditions, the views of the local police authorities and the demands made on the police by the local inhabitants would not be satisfactory. The Geddes' recommendation was, therefore, not implemented. But it was recognised that there was a case for rather more central supervision of the strengths of police forces than had been exercised before, not only in order to safeguard the Exchequer by restraining any police authority which policed its area on too generous a basis or adopted an extravagant organisation, but also to secure the maintenance of sufficient numbers for efficient policing. Fairly close control over strengths is therefore now exercised. Changes in strengths are normally discussed at some length by the Chief Constable, H.M. Inspector, and the police authority before they are submitted to the Home Office for approval, but in spite of fairly elaborate machinery for determining the size of each force, and in spite of the fact that the Home Secretary has substantial powers to enforce his will, one still finds considerable variations in the sizes of forces policing similar types of area. For much depends on the view of the police authority and Chief Constable. The Home Office does not lay down any yardstick which has to be applied to similar areas: rather it works on the proposals made by the local people, using them as its basis. Of course it often insists on more or fewer men than the police authority proposes, but it does not do this to such an extent that uniformity is secured throughout the country. If it did, the pattern of policing would be much more symmetrical than it is. Moreover, the different Inspectors do not always apply the same standards in this matter, and whilst the Home Office tries to see that they do, this is not always easy.

Interference by the Home Secretary with the police authority's choice of Chief Constable has recently been a subject of bitter controversy. Since 1839 it has been necessary for a county police authority to obtain the Home Secretary's approval to their choice of Chief Constable, but for many years this was given more or less automatically, except on one or two occasions when the police authority proposed to appoint a 'ranker.'

The Home Secretary's approval of the choice of Chief Constable by borough police authorities was not required until 1920. The regulation of that year which required this and which still operates both for counties and boroughs is as follows:

'Every appointment to the post of chief officer of police of any county or borough force shall be subject to the approval of the Secretary of State, and no person without previous police experience shall be appointed to any such post unless he possesses some exceptional qualification or experience which specially fits him for the post, or there is no candidate from the police service who is considered sufficiently well qualified.'

This regulation was made following a recommendation of the Desborough Committee who seem to have contemplated that the Home Secretary would be more than a rubber stamp, as they recommended that, when coming to a decision, he should have before him particulars of the qualifications and experience of all the candidates on the short list, that is, of those from whom the final selection was made. In spite of this recommendation, the police authority's choice seems to have been approved automatically during the years between the wars, provided the condition regarding previous police experience was fulfilled. Several of the appointments were severely criticised in the House of Commons, some of them, as it proved later, with justification, but on each occasion the Home Secretary said that if the appointment was within the terms of the regulations, it was not his function to veto it. He had 'merely to approve of it'; he was 'bound to appoint' a candidate if he complied with the regulations; he was not the appointing, but only the confirming authority; it was 'quite impossible for him to attempt to control these appointments'; it was not his duty. The same policy was followed by Labour and Conservative Home Secretaries. For example, Mr. Clynes, in 1931, said, 'It is not part of my duty to enter into details of other applicants. My function is limited to sanctioning after the proper authority has dealt with the appointment.'

The procedure followed in making these appointments was not altogether satisfactory. Often the post was not advertised; even if it was advertised, the best candidates were not always included on the short list; sometimes H.M. Inspector's advice would be sought; sometimes it would not; even if he was consulted, he would often know little about candidates who were not already Chief Constables. But the worst feature of the system was that the appointment was in the hands of a committee, often too large for the purpose, many of whose members would have little or no experience in the skilled task of interviewing candidates for a responsible post, and some of whom were not free from prejudice and partisanship of one kind or another. They would often make up their minds on insufficient information after a short interview with a few applicants.

B.P.   F

It is not surprising, therefore, that during the war, when the weakest links in the chain began to show up, the Home Secretary came to take rather more interest in these appointments. He had, it is true, powers under the Defence Regulations to require a Chief Constable to retire if he did not consider him fit to perform his duties, but it was obviously better to try to avoid difficulties by preventing the appointment of unsuitable men. Police authorities were, therefore, in 1941, asked to advertise vacant posts of Chief Constable. The Home Secretary then asked to see the short list of candidates; he would take H.M. Inspectors' views on it and pass them on to the police authority. Sometimes he would suggest that another name should be added to the candidates for interview; sometimes he would inform the police authority that he would not in any event be prepared to approve Mr. X, or any local candidate if he thought the force needed new blood.

Some police authorities welcomed the assistance of the Home Office and Inspectors in choosing a new Chief Constable; others did not. They argued that they were in a better position than the Home Secretary and his officials to select the best man, and that in any event he had not got the right to interfere with their discretion. The best example of a dispute on these lines is the case of Salford which occurred in 1947. The Home Secretary refused to approve the Watch Committee's choice of the deputy as Chief Constable, and it was not until he threatened to withhold the relatively large sum of £100,000 from the Exchequer grant, that the Committee rescinded its decision and chose a man who was acceptable to the Home Secretary. Passions ran high whilst the matter was at issue. The Home Secretary's action was described as the 'vicious bludgeoning of the Salford people into submission to the dictates of a Minister'. It was suggested that he had no statutory right to disqualify a person from appointment as a Chief Constable on the ground that the candidate had not served in another force, and that even if he had the right he should not presume to know better than the local people. The incident was regarded in many quarters as one more example of monstrous interference by bureaucrats in Whitehall with the exercise by police authorities of their discretion. The Home Secretary justified his action on the ground that the law placed a certain responsibility on him and that he had to discharge it in accordance with his conscience. The previous Chief Constable had held the post for a long time and he thought new blood should be introduced. In any event he did not regard the deputy as personally suitable for the post of Chief Constable. Whether or not he was suitable, the matter was undoubtedly badly handled. The Home Office did not make it clear from the start that the Home Secretary would not approve the deputy, and the Home Secretary should either not have given the reasons for his decision or stuck to the same ones throughout.

There is also some justification in the complaint that the Home Office has not been consistent in its policy during the last few years: the procedure has been haphazard and this has inevitably given the impression that the Home Secretary was acting in an arbitrary way. If he proposes to be more than a rubber stamp, he should require all short lists to be submitted to him and time to be allowed for his views to be expressed. It would also save trouble and embarrassment if appointments were not announced in the Press before he has confirmed them, but this could presumably not be done by a police regulation and in any event might be thought an infringement of the liberty of the Press. On the other hand, it would not be appropriate for the Home Secretary, as is sometimes suggested, to work to some hard and fast rule: the circumstances vary so greatly from time to time and from force to force that in some cases it may be appropriate to appoint a local candidate and in others it may not.

The extent to which the Home Secretary should control appointments to the post of Chief Constable is bound to be a controversial issue. If local police authorities are to remain responsible for maintaining police forces in their districts and are to have more than a shadow of power, they must clearly be allowed a considerable measure of discretion in selecting their Chief Officers of police; but there is little doubt that the appointments made in the past have often left much to be desired. Nor is the problem inconsiderable, as on an average 12 to 15 appointments are made each year. It is unlikely that first-rate men will be appointed to the head of every force unless police authorities are given and take expert advice from those who are in a position to know more about the candidates than they do, and who should be able to take a more detached view of the matter and to help them in surveying the needs of their area and the field of selection. The ideal arrangement would therefore be for the

Home Secretary to insist that the post is advertised, and that he sees the short list of candidates for interview prepared by the police authority as well as the names of all the applicants. He should then inform the authority of any candidates on the short list whose appointment he would not approve, require the addition of other names to the list if he thinks this desirable, and leave the police authority free to choose from the candidates on the list. In some cases the police authority might also ask the Home Secretary to give his detailed views on the candidates or to put them in order of merit, and sometimes the Home Secretary might feel disposed to do this even if not requested. It would seem that an arrangement on these lines would secure a reasonable compromise between the local and central authorities and secure the appointment of better men than have at times been appointed in the past, whilst leaving a considerable measure of discretion to police authorities.

Disciplinary Appeals

Discipline is, it will be recalled, one of the matters dealt with in the Home Secretary's regulations. These regulations prescribe the offences against discipline for which a member of a police force may be punished, the procedure (in considerable detail) which is to be followed in such cases, and the punishments which may be inflicted. The Home Secretary also has certain appellate functions in connection with discipline. Under the Police (Appeals) Acts, 1927 and 1943, a member of a police force who is dismissed or required to resign or reduced in rank or pay, is entitled to appeal to the Home Secretary. No appeal lies against minor punishments, but this has been recommended by the Oaksey Committee. The relevant documents must be submitted to the Home Secretary who, unless he decides that the case can properly be determined without taking oral evidence, is required to appoint one or more persons to hold an enquiry and report to him. One at least of the persons holding the enquiry must be engaged or experienced in police work. There is no requirement that the report shall be published. Nor is the Home Secretary bound by any recommendation made in the report: he is free to allow or to dismiss the appeal or to vary the punishment by reducing or increasing it as he sees fit. In fact, enquiries have been held in only a minority of cases.

The Desborough Committee recommended that there should be

a right of appeal against dismissal and that the appeal should lie to a barrister of standing or a judge, with one of H.M. Inspectors as assessor on technical matters. The Government, when it came to legislate on this matter, preferred an appeal to the Home Secretary. There is certainly much to be said for this decision. For in an appeal of this kind the appellate body must not only review the evidence, consider any fresh evidence and determine the facts; it must also decide whether the punishment should be varied. This can only properly be done in the light of experience of police work. The kind of question to be determined is whether it is safe and expedient to leave in the police a man who has committed a criminal offence; whether certain conduct was prejudicial to discipline; whether it was reasonable to dismiss a man who married without permission; whether a superior officer abused his powers. It would seem that the Home Office is more fitted to advise the Home Secretary on this kind of issue than is an *ad hoc* tribunal of outsiders, even if assisted by a technical assessor.

A striking change has occurred in recent years in the proportion of appeals allowed. Between 1927 and 1935 one appeal (and that from a Chief Constable) out of the 103 made was allowed, though in three the punishment was reduced; whereas between 1936 and 1947, 13 out of 107 appeals were allowed. Who is to say how these figures are to be explained? Have the local disciplinary authorities—Chief Constables and Watch Committees—been less careful in investigating the facts and in determining punishments, or has the Home Secretary been more liberal, more sympathetic to the lower ranks in his administration of the discipline code? Different answers will probably be given to these questions and to the question whether the system works fairly, according to the standpoint of the person answering. Our chief concern here is to draw attention to the Home Secretary's powers as the appellate body in all but minor discipline cases. There is no appeal to the ordinary courts, either against the local disciplinary authority's decision, or against the Home Secretary's, though in certain circumstances it is possible to bring before a court an issue such as whether the disciplinary authority had any jurisdiction. But an insufficient proportion of cases in which there is a right of appeal come before the Home Secretary (probably never more than 10 per cent. each year) for one to be able to say that his appellate powers enable him to secure a reasonable measure of uniformity in the administration of discipline by Chief Officers and police authorities, and there are, as the Oaksey Committee has shown, wide divergences in the way discipline is administered from force to force, and as between various types of force.

Inspection

The Home Secretary is considerably aided in his task of supervising the police service of the country by His Majesty's Inspectors of Constabulary. The duties of these inspectors are laid down in the County and Borough Police Act, 1856. They are 'to visit and inquire into the state and the efficiency of the police appointed for every county and borough, and whether the provisions of the Acts under which such police are appointed are duly observed and carried into effect, and also into the state of police stations, charge rooms, cells, or lock ups, or other premises occupied for the use of such police.'

The Inspectors do not inspect the Metropolitan police force and have never done so. Nor are they required or authorised by statute to inspect the City of London force, but since 1919, when the Government first contributed towards the cost of this force, it has been inspected. It would appear that inspection of the City of London force is less thorough than that of the county and borough forces, being confined to one very formal inspection a year, but it is difficult for an outsider to inform himself about this as the published reports of the Inspectors normally say no more about the City of London police force than that 'the conditions upon which the Exchequer contribution is made have been satisfied.' Each Inspector normally inspects every force in the district to which he has been assigned once a year, but he will also visit most of the forces on other occasions, and if a force is in trouble of some kind, he will be in constant touch with the Chief Constable and also probably with the chairman and clerk of the police authority.

The Inspectors concern themselves with almost every aspect of police organisation and work: the strength of the force, with particular regard to its adequacy; the allocation of the work and the responsibilities given to the various ranks; police buildings and houses; methods of communication, i.e. police cars, wireless, telephone boxes, etc.; the maintenance of discipline; training; equipment; uniforms; and last, but not least, the methods and success of the force in preventing and detecting crime. They also keep an eye on the way matters raised by the Police Federation have been handled locally and will themselves see any member of the force who wishes to raise some matter with them, not always, though often, in the presence of the Chief Constable. By their knowledge of what happens in other forces, they are often able to give useful advice to Chief Constables, and they are, of course, constantly asked by the Home Secretary to advise him both on particular points of police administration affecting individual forces, and on general questions affecting the police service as a whole from the value of police dogs to the need for a police college. Their usefulness in these regards would be enhanced if they inspected the Metropolitan police force, and not merely two-thirds of the police strength of the country.

From time to time there has been a tendency for inspections to become rather superficial. Sir Leonard Dunning, in his report for 1919, said that the issue of certificates of efficiency had been a matter of routine for some years. This was also admitted in the evidence given by the Home Office witness before the Royal Commission on Local Government in 1923; moreover, in his view the Inspectors had not always taken full advantage of their unique opportunities of comparing methods of organisation in different forces and inducing the backward forces to drop their antiquated methods. Recently there has been evidence that the Inspectors know more about what is happening and play a more positive rôle. This may be partly due to the fact that there are more of them now than there were. Most Inspectors to-day regard the less formal side as the more important, and spend much of their time probing into such things as the use of man-power, deficiencies in equipment, the administration of discipline and any alleged irregularities. They will also discuss with the Chief Constable and with members of the police authority in a frank and friendly way the main problems with which they are concerned at that time. This must be emphasised: otherwise the term 'inspection' will give a false impression.

The Act of 1856 required each of the Inspectors to report generally upon the matters into which he had to inquire to the Secretary of State who was to lay such reports before Parliament. Until 1914 the reports which were laid before Parliament were composed of a general report by each of the Inspectors and of their detailed reports on each of the forces. It might be thought that this would have given Parliament and the public a good picture of the state of the police service. It did at first, but soon the reports became stereotyped: one finds the same formulæ repeated year after year, and very few general comments of interest. Since 1914 the reports made by the Inspectors on each of the forces in their districts have not been published. They are submitted to the Home Secretary who takes appropriate action on them. This is probably a better system than the previous one, as any published comments made on an individual force are likely to be guarded, and the present system should not inhibit the Inspector from making a frank report to the Home Secretary. Since 1945 a further change has been made. In lieu of one report by each of the Inspectors, a composite report, which is laid before Parliament, has been submitted by all the Inspectors together. This makes it easier to obtain a coherent picture of what is happening in the police, and for Parliament and the public to inform themselves on the matter and to offer effective criticisms on the issues on which they are necessary. Even so the annual reports of the Inspectors tell one remarkably little. They are brief—averaging before 1949 12 to 15 pages—and they appear usually to be putting the best possible face on everything. There are occasional hints of certain shortcomings: police authorities should make greater efforts to house their men; those in positions of leadership must adjust themselves to current changes in human relations; but generally speaking the strong rather than the weak points of the service are emphasised and the future is looked forward to with confidence. It may be objected that it was never intended that the Inspectors should do anything different in their reports. This may be, but the result is that it is difficult for persons outside the service to know much about it. Incidentally it is not clear what the position would be if an Inspector wished to publish in his report something to which the Home Secretary took exception.

Financial Control

The ultimate sanction behind most other forms of control over police authorities is financial. If they refuse to comply with the Home Secretary's regulations, if they choose a Chief Constable

who is not acceptable to him, if they fail to appoint enough policemen, or to maintain discipline impartially and properly, in the last
resort when all other methods have failed the Home Secretary can
withhold the Government grant in aid of police expenditure. It is
like a resort to force between nations, and as one of the parties is
much stronger than the other, it always wins.

The Exchequer grant to police authorities is equal to one-half of
all their approved expenditure on police purposes. In administering
this grant the Home Secretary is not tied by any statutory conditions. In fact it is often said that the police grant is non-statutory.
It is in a sense, but the statement is misleading unless it is remembered that Parliament sanctions the expenditure of so many pounds
every year in the Appropriation Act, for *inter alia* police purposes,
having had estimates submitted to it earlier. Nevertheless, it remains
true that the Home Secretary has a very free hand in administering
the police grant. The only conditions governing its payment are
laid down in rules made by the Home Secretary himself with the
approval of the Treasury. These rules provide that he may withhold the grant in whole or in part if he is not satisfied that the police
service is efficiently and properly administered or if his approval
has not been obtained for the rates of pay and allowances of the
force.

But before we examine control through the Exchequer grant, we
must examine control through the audit. This is exercised as much
in the interests of the local ratepayer as in those of the central
government. In the counties expenditure on the police is audited
as part of the accounts of county councils which are all required by
statute to be audited by the District Auditors of the Ministry of
Health. The auditor will not only see that the accounts have been
properly kept and that there has been no embezzlement or dis-
honest practices; he will also scrutinise them to see that all expenditure has been authorised by statute or regulation or specifically by
the Home Secretary; but he is not concerned with the wisdom of
expenditure. He has power to disallow illegal expenditure and sur-
charge it on those responsible, unless retrospective approval is
secured from the Ministry of Health, and he would report to the
Home Office anything irregular if it affected the claim for police
grant. In the boroughs the position is different. In the majority of
cases, there is no statutory requirement that the accounts shall be

audited by the District Auditor, but the Home Office requires that
they shall be examined by him in connection with the claim to
grant. He certifies that he has examined the accounts and the claim
to Government grant, that to the best of his knowledge and belief
the accounts are correct and that subject to his report, if any, the
entries in the claim contain no charge which is not in accordance
with the Home Secretary's rules. He has not got power to disallow
any illegal expenditure. The accounts of combined police authorities are all audited by the District Auditors.

The next step is for the claims for grant to be submitted to the
Home Office. Much detail has to be submitted concerning some of
the expenditure of police authorities, e.g. on pensions, and the
Home Office will check every pension and allowance paid down to
the last penny, pursuing relentlessly any authority which does not
agree with its view as to the correct sum. On other matters comparatively little detail is submitted with claims for police grant and
large sums of money are passed with little investigation. The
justification for these differences is not apparent.*

Where an unauthorised payment is discovered, the matter will be
taken up with the police authority who will be asked to explain
their action, and unless they can do so satisfactorily, the amount paid
in excess of the authorised figure will be disallowed for grant. The
excess already paid will, unless recovered from the recipient, probably be borne by the police fund of the police authority who will be
asked by the Home Office to see that no overpayments are made in
future. Sometimes the police authority may think inadequate the
amount authorised by statute or regulation or by the Home Office,
and will wish to pay more even if Government grant is not forthcoming on the higher amount, but the Home Office will try to
prevent this, if necessary by threatening to withhold grant on other
items of expenditure. It is sometimes suggested that police authorities should be allowed to do what they like on such matters provided
the excess payment is borne by the rates, but the Home Secretary
considers that he has a duty to see that the law relating to the

* Since this was written, proposals to eliminate much of the detail required in
claims for police grant and to give police authorities greater freedom in connection
with police buildings have been made in the First Report of the Local Government
Manpower Committee (Cmd. 7870). Further relaxation is foreshadowed. Although
these steps do not go far enough for some critics, they are a marked and welcome
step forward.

administration of the police is properly applied, and any other course would probably have an unsettling effect on the police and lead to the type of difficulty which was encountered before 1919 when there were wide differences in conditions of service.

Where a police authority proposes to spend money on some matter which is not governed by statute or regulation or by specific Home Office authority, it will in all probability submit its proposals to the Home Office to obtain prior approval. This would happen in connection, for instance, with any new building. The plans of police stations or police houses which an authority proposed to erect would be submitted to the Home Office and examined with some care before approval was given and half the cost allowed to rank for Exchequer grant. The approval of the Ministry of Health would also have to be obtained. A similar procedure would be followed if any authority proposed to make an *ex gratia* payment to someone who had a grievance against the police, or if it was about to incur legal costs in connection with some action brought against a member of the force. Where, as in some instances, money has been spent on some exceptional matter of this kind before reference to the Home Office, retrospective approval may be given and the sum involved allowed to rank for grant if it appears reasonable.

The control over expenditure described above is not as spectacular as the instances which occur from time to time of the withholding of large sums not merely on some item of expenditure which has been disallowed, but as an instrument to induce a police authority to take, or to refrain from taking, some action. It is not easy for an outsider to get a complete picture of the occasions on which grant has been used as an instrument of persuasion as there is no systematic method of publishing the facts. In some cases they come out in Parliament or the Press; in others, for no apparent reason, they do not. But the number of occasions on which the Home Office has applied this sanction during the last 20 years does not probably exceed ten or twelve.

The most usual ground for withholding grant has probably been the refusal of an authority to bring its force up to the strength recommended by the Home Office. The severity of the penalty can be illustrated by the case of Brighton in July, 1939. The authority were informed that their grant would be reduced by almost one-quarter until they increased their force by 3 per cent. (seven men). Within three days they had reversed their decision which had been adhered to for months. It may appear strange to withhold grant in order to make an authority spend more money, but it is difficult to see how else the Home Secretary could secure that a force was brought up to the strength he considered necessary. If a police authority insisted on maintaining a larger force than the Home Secretary approved, grant would at first probably be withheld only on the unauthorised men. If this did not produce the required result, grant would probably be withheld on authorised expenditure as well, but it is rare for this to happen. Sometimes grant has been withheld in order to persuade an authority to build a new police station, or, as in the Salford case, in connection with the appointment of a Chief Constable. In 1944 it was used when a Watch Committee had, in the Home Secretary's view, failed to appreciate their responsibility as the disciplinary authority for the force; at the same time the Home Secretary refused to approve the appointment of a member of the force as Chief Constable on the ground that the appointment should have been made from outside the force; the Watch Committee resigned in protest; the Town Council elected another Committee; another Chief Constable was in due course chosen and the Exchequer grant was restored when the Home Secretary was satisfied that the force was being efficiently maintained and properly administered.

If, as appears to be the case, the Home Secretary is prepared to withhold all grant in aid from a police authority indefinitely, it is obvious that the weapon will be effective, and it is therefore very important to try to ensure that this tremendous power is not abused. It may be asked whether this is secured under the present system. The Public Accounts Committee has from time to time expressed the view that where it is desired that continuing functions should be exercised by a Government Department, particularly where such functions may involve financial liabilities extending beyond a given financial year, it is proper, subject to certain recognised exceptions, that the powers and duties to be exercised should be defined by specific statute. The Treasury agrees generally with this principle, but considers that it is clearly within the right of Parliament to provide grants on the authority of the Appropriation Acts even though they relate to continuing services. The opportunity of the Police (Scotland) Act, 1946, was taken to put the Scottish police grant on a statutory basis, and the Public Accounts Committee has expressed regret that similar authority for corresponding but much larger grants for the police in England and Wales was not included in the Police Act, 1946.

It is too soon yet to say whether the Scottish provision will alter in any material way the administration of the police grant. The grants are, in the words of the statute, to consist of 'such sums [paid] at such times, in such manner, and subject to such conditions as the Secretary of State may with the approval of the Treasury by order determine'. The Police Grant (Scotland) Order, 1947, which was made under the Act leaves a great deal to the determination of the Secretary of State for Scotland, and authorises him, if he is not satisfied on a wide range of matters, to withhold grant in whole or in part permanently or for such time as he may determine. An order made under the regulation has, it is true, to be laid before Parliament, but it is only subject to a negative resolution, and it seems unlikely that Parliament will have any more control over the administration of the Scottish police grant than it had before. The position may be slightly more satisfactory from the point of view of police authorities; but on the whole this seems unlikely. The steps taken no doubt meet the objections raised by the Public Accounts Committee by providing a continuing statutory backing for a continuing service, but it seems improbable that they will do more than this.

If any reform is to be made in the English system, it would seem more effective to do it by limiting the Home Secretary's discretion to withhold grant; but it is very difficult to devise a workable solution. There would be great technical difficulties in imposing certain maxima or requiring that the amount withheld bore some authorised relation to the cost of the item at issue. It would, for instance, be impossible to foresee all eventualities. And would one have a penalty at one rate for non-compliance with a statute and at another rate for non-compliance with a regulation? What if the former raised a much less important issue than the latter? And how would one determine what the maximum should be where the issue at stake was the appointment of a Chief Constable? The present system, acting as it does more as a stimulant to spending than as a curb on extravagance, is no doubt not altogether satisfactory from the point of view of police authorities, but it does ensure that on the whole an efficient police service is maintained, and it may be that this is the only way to ensure it.

Parliamentary Control

Normally the more responsibility a Minister has for something, the easier it is for Parliament to supervise it. Thus if appeals in police disciplinary cases lay to a special tribunal or to a court and not to the Home Secretary, it would not be possible to question in Parliament the decision on an appeal. The Home Secretary will probably not be prepared to discuss the grounds for his decision in any particular case, but the matter can at least be raised and he will very likely indicate the general considerations which he has in mind when determining such appeals.

But parliamentary control over the Home Secretary's administration of the provincial police has not kept pace with the growth in his powers and his use of them. Thus Parliament can question the Home Secretary about any aspect of the administration and conduct of the Metropolitan police, and he is bound to answer, since he, as police authority, is responsible; but he will not usually answer questions about provincial police forces on matters for which he does not consider himself responsible. It is, of course, very difficult to say what 'responsibility' means, or should mean, in this connection. The Speaker of the House of Commons usually interprets it rather narrowly, but different rulings have been given at different times. For example, in 1926 the Speaker ruled that 'matters which are under the control of local authorities must be dealt with by those local authorities, and not here on the floor of the House. . . . It would never do to bring up here matters which have their remedy in another place' (meaning the Council Chamber, not the House of Lords). But in subsequent discussion, the Speaker agreed that where the Minister had an overriding power, or, as in the case of the police, the service was inspected by his officers and half of the cost borne by the Exchequer, questions might be allowed.

In 1935, in a debate on the Home Office Estimates, a Member of Parliament drew attention to the action taken by the police at a meeting in South Wales. The Chairman ruled this out of order: 'The mere fact,' he said, 'that the House of Commons grants money for certain purposes does not necessarily put the responsibility for carrying out that service on the shoulders of His Majesty's Government. In some cases it does; in some it does not. In this case the statute law specifically lays it down that it is the responsibility of the local authority.' There was no responsibility on the Home Office, which was solely responsible for the Metropolitan police force. Members should not even cite examples from forces other than the Metropolitan police. Later, however, he admitted that the Home Office had a responsibility to see that the police service was efficient.

What was meant by 'responsibility for efficiency' was explained by the Speaker in 1936 during a debate on the banning of a political meeting by a Chief Constable. The Home Secretary was responsible for seeing that when the police were inspected they came up to certain standards of efficiency; he could not withhold grant because the police banned meetings; he could not give the police orders and was therefore not responsible for them; the police authority had 'absolute control over the provincial police'; the most the Home Secretary could do was to circularise local authorities and give them advice; on the Home Office vote, members could discuss suggestions the Home Secretary had made or not made to police authorities, but not whether his advice had been followed, as he was not responsible for this. This view was hotly contested by many members; they argued that the test of efficiency was in action. It was ridiculous that they could raise with the Home Office the fact that a force was insufficiently clad or had bad teeth, but not that the police behaved improperly at a political meeting. The Speaker stuck to his ruling; how the police carried out their duty was a matter for the police authority, not for the Home Secretary, who was concerned only with seeing they were efficient, that is, properly drilled, trained and clothed. One gets the impression incidentally throughout this debate that the Speaker thought that the system of certificates of efficiency, which was abolished in 1929, still obtained.

The Home Secretary himself usually takes a less narrow view of his responsibilities. He will normally enquire into serious allegations that the police have behaved improperly, and when necessary take some further action. Legally he may have no power to do this, but in fact he has. He might send an Inspector down to talk to the Chief Constable, or summon the Chief Constable to Whitehall. A committee of enquiry might be appointed and, although its findings would not be binding on anyone, it would assist the Home Secretary in criticising the actions of the police if this were necessary. In a very bad case, grant would probably be withheld. This would most likely not be done ostensibly on account of the behaviour of the police to the public, but because the Home Secretary was not satisfied with the way in which discipline was being administered by the Chief Constable or police authority. Most Home Secretaries know that it does not satisfy the House of Commons to be told, when they are complaining about the behaviour of the police at strikes or political meetings, that the matter is no concern of his and that any aggrieved person may seek his remedy by suing the police officers in question. Nor would they be satisfied if, when complaining about some improper behaviour of a Chief Constable, the Home Secretary simply replied that this was the affair of the local police authority. He does, however, usually draw a line at trying to get uniformity in the way the police enforce the law. Thus there were many complaints between the wars at the way the police enforced the traffic laws and demands for more uniform action, but the Home Secretary always refused to interfere.

Members of Parliament seem often to want the best of both worlds: full 'democratic' control by the local police authority and no interference from Whitehall, and at the same time the right to raise any matter in the House of Commons and to hold some Minister responsible for it. It is not easy to reconcile the two things. It seems doubtful, however, whether public opinion would be satisfied if the Home Secretary abided by the Speaker's strict rulings. When so much public money is contributed towards a service, the taxpayer wants to be assured that it is free of abuses and functions satisfactorily, as well as looking efficient when inspected.

Prosecutions

In most countries, including Scotland, the police are investigators, but not, except to a limited extent, prosecutors, the duty of deciding whether or not to prosecute, and of prosecuting, in criminal cases being laid on a State prosecuting authority. In England and Wales, on the other hand, criminal proceedings are Crown prosecutions only in the formal sense that they are all in the name of the King, all crimes being offences against the 'King's Peace': in fact the police and not the Crown initiate most prosecutions. They decide whether or not to prosecute and in most cases conduct the prosecution, though where the offence is serious the police will take legal advice and be legally represented. This arrangement is a matter of practice and is not prescribed by law. As Sir J. Moylan says in 'The Police of Britain': 'In some cases the police prosecute in pursuance of a statutory provision, but in general their legal status is only that of the common informer, a rôle which any citizen may fill but which, as a matter of custom and practice, is left to the police'.

But the freedom of each local Chief Constable in the matter of prosecutions is to some extent limited by the Director of Public Prosecutions. The Director is appointed by the Home Secretary, but is in all matters under the control of the Attorney General. He is required by regulations to take charge (1) where the offence is punishable by death, (2) when a case is referred to him by a Government Department (subject to his discretion), and (3) in any case 'which appears to him to be of importance or difficulty or which for any other reason requires his intervention.' He may give advice to, *inter alia*, Chief Constables in any criminal matter which he considers important or difficult, and the police are required to report to him many classes of offences. He is in this way able to obtain full information, and he has a wide discretion to give advice in such cases as he thinks desirable. Though the number of cases dealt with by the Director forms only a very small proportion of the total of criminal prosecutions, his power and influence are probably greater now than they have been at any time before 1946, when the regulations governing his functions and duties were revised (S.R. & O. 1946, No. 1467/L.17).

There is, nevertheless, still an important difference between the position in England and in other countries. The most the Home Secretary does is to explain new statutes to Chief Constables, with perhaps an indication of what he conceives to be the intentions of Parliament in making a particular law, and he might occasionally advise them not to enforce some antique statute. It would be rare for the Home Secretary to suggest that prosecutions might or might not be instituted in such and such circumstances or against a particular class of offender, whether in political or other cases, and in any event there is no action he can take if his advice is ignored. Nor does the Director give advice to the police on what may be called matters of Government policy, though he would on legal issues. Apart from those cases in which the Director has power to take over or to

interfere, there is no machinery for securing that the law is put into
action on any uniform policy in England and Wales.

Centrally Run Services

It has been found necessary during recent years to supplement,
by centrally run services, the services which the local police authorities provided in connection with such things as technical aids to the
detection of crime and the training of the police.

The police have made increasing use recently of scientific aids
in the detection of crime, but it is obviously unnecessary and too
expensive for each force to have its own scientific staff and a labora-
tory. During the last ten years or so, therefore, the Home Office has
established laboratories for the use of regional groups of forces.
The staff of the laboratories, which consists mostly of scientists,
not of police officers, is appointed by the Home Office by whom the
service is administered, subject to a certain degree of control
by representatives of police authorities. Some Chief Constables
were at first slow to appreciate the use of these forensic science
laboratories, and preferred their force to do their own scientific
work or to consult outside specialists who had previously assisted
them; others doubted the value of scientific aids altogether; but
on the whole the laboratories were quickly appreciated and have
been a great success. The financial arrangements which were
adopted encouraged their use, as police authorities wished to get
something in return for the contributions they all had to make.
The laboratories do some research as well as day-to-day work for
the police.

Similar arrangements were made shortly before 1939 for a
regional wireless service to be used by groups of police forces.
Wireless stations were set up, staffed and administered by the Home
Office and paid for in the same way as the forensic science laboratories. For various technical reasons they were not a success and
have now been abolished, but the Home Office continues to own
and to 'service' all the wireless equipment of forces.

More recently still, arrangements on rather similar lines have been
made for the training of recruits and of the higher ranks at a police
college. Several district training schools for recruits were set up
by the Home Office at the end of the second world war and are still

in existence. The Chief Constables and police authorities in each district take part in the management of the schools. More will be said about the training schools and the police college in a later chapter, but they are mentioned here as examples of services which are not run by the individual forces.

The way in which the laboratories and training establishments are financed is of some interest. They are paid for initially by the Home Office, but about half the cost is reclaimed from police authorities, not according to the use they make of the services, but according to the strength of each force. Estimates of the total cost of the services are made by the Home Office and placed before a committee largely composed of representatives of police authorities which is known as the Central Committee on Police Special Services. The Committee examines the estimates and amends them as it sees fit. It then fixes the contribution to be paid by police authorities for each policeman they are authorised to employ. This also includes the cost of wireless maintenance. The contribution is deducted from the Exchequer grant paid to each force.

Devices such as these enable a higher standard of technical efficiency to be attained than would be possible if in such matters each force was left to do the best it could in combination or not as it saw fit with other forces. These regional services are, of course, of greatest use to the smaller forces who have less resources at their disposal than the larger ones. It would be putting it too high to say that they have given a new lease of life to the present structure of the police service, but they are certainly a useful way of counteracting the weaknesses due to the existence of 129 separate forces without impairing the essential features of local control. Arrangements such as these usually create suspicions amongst those who automatically see Whitehall as the enemy. For instance, a recent article in the *Economist* stated that 'the trend towards centralisation which this change [the establishment of recruit-training schools] suggests is not so sinister as might appear.'

The total cost of these special services during the financial year 1948–1949 was £797,000, about three-eighths of which was contributed by police authorities. The total cost of the police in that year was nearly £42 million, so it will be seen that the special services represent only a very small fraction (less than one-fiftieth) of the whole.

Other Contacts and Controls

No account of the rôle played by the central authority would be complete without mention of the less formal methods by which the police service is supervised and guided. First and perhaps most important are the personal contacts between the Home Office and Chief Constables. It is sometimes suggested that directly established relations between a local government officer and a central department are undesirable because the central department may give orders to the officer behind the back of the authority he serves. Whether such fears are justified or not, few people would dispute that it is good for the official in Whitehall to be confronted with the object of his attentions. This should prevent him becoming too theoretical and should give him valuable first-hand information about the service he is administering, besides being a constant reminder that many things differ from place to place. Such contacts develop a relation of partnership rather than one of control: the official is less likely to issue peremptory, authoritarian instructions if he knows personally the man to whom he is writing, and the Chief Constable will better appreciate the sort of considerations which have to be taken into account when a decision of national and not merely local importance is being made, if the matter has been talked over freely and frankly with the persons responsible for making the decision. These contacts have been emphasised because it seems probable that they are rather closer than the usual contacts between local government officers and the central department. There has been a long tradition of such personal contacts in the police service, and most police authorities would expect their Chief Constable to keep in fairly close touch with the Home Office, though some would guard more closely than others against the danger of the Chief Constable regarding Whitehall and not the police authority as his master.

Rather more formal relations with Chief Constables are maintained through the machinery of their District and Central Conferences. These conferences, which started in 1917, have no statutory basis or functions, but are a useful piece of administrative machinery. Originally they were intended to enable Chief Constables to discuss amongst themselves and with Government officials matters arising from the executive duties of the police, and they are still used for this purpose, particularly to discuss the more intricate parts of the criminal law; but in recent years they have concerned themselves also with pay and conditions of service.

There is no corresponding machinery for consultations with police authorities, apart from the Police Council. Home Office officials will, of course, always be prepared to see the clerk or chairman or other members of a police authority on any issue they wish to raise. But clerks do not maintain such close contacts with the Home Office as Chief Constables, though they often ask for advice on legal issues connected with the administration of the police. The Police Committees of the County Councils Association and Association of Municipal Corporations have for many years been accepted as the representative organisations of county and borough police authorities respectively. No association of magistrates is consulted by the Home Secretary regarding the administration of the police, in the same way as he consults the local authority associations, in spite of the fact that Standing Joint Committees are composed half of magistrates and that the justices also have certain powers over the executive actions of the police.

It would, however, be absurd to suggest that most advice to police authorities and Chief Constables is given orally. There is the well-worn practice of issuing a circular letter which may go to all police authorities, or to all Chief Constables, or to both. Since 1919, when the Home Secretary was given greatly increased powers in connection with the police, the Home Office has inevitably issued many more circulars than it did previously, culminating in several hundred a year during the war of 1939–1945 to the dismay of some of the recipients. These circulars cover a great range of subjects. They may draw attention to new legislation of interest to the police, or explain the effect of legal decisions or the meaning of statutes or orders which the police will have to enforce. Other circulars may ask police authorities to review some matter such as the strength of their forces in the light of an emergency, or to estimate their housing needs. Others announce changes in the police regulations or give advice about the administration of the police discipline code. Most of these circulars are concerned with the administration of the police, e.g. their conditions of service, rather than with their executive actions. The distinction between control over these two types of matter is of fundamental importance and will be discussed in the concluding chapter.

CHAPTER V

The Rôle of the Local Authority

Some Limitations to Central Control

THE emphasis in the preceding chapter was inevitably placed on the limitations to the powers of local police authorities resulting from central controls, and it is desirable to remember that the statutory duty to establish police forces rests, outside the Metropolitan police district, not on the Home Secretary but on the local police authorities. Thus in the counties the combined effect of the County and Borough Police Act, 1856, and the Local Government Act, 1888, is to require the justices in Quarter Sessions and county council jointly to establish a sufficient police force for each county; and in the boroughs the Municipal Corporations Act, 1882, as amended, requires the Watch Committee of every county borough council to appoint a sufficient number of fit men to be borough constables. Similarly if two or more police authorities combine or are combined by the Home Secretary, the amalgamation scheme must provide that the combined police authority shall establish and maintain a combined force for the combined area.

If no police force were appointed in some locality, the Home Secretary would not have power as the law stands to appoint and maintain one himself. He might conceivably, though improbably, as a temporary measure send a contingent from the Metropolitan police force to keep order in the district, but there would be grave difficulties in any such arrangement, and it is unlikely that he would be able thus to misuse for long the resources of the Metropolitan police fund. This illustrates the point that only the local police authority has the power to establish and maintain a force and the responsibility to do so. It is they who must decide how many men (and women) they need properly to police their area and how many there should be in each of the ranks, and, in counties, in each of the districts. These decisions are, it is true, subject to the Home Secretary's approval, but they are made in the first instance by the local police authority, who thus have an opportunity to take any relevant local considerations into account and to make out a case for the policing of their area on the scale they fancy.

Having appointed their force, the police authority must pay them. The scales on which they are to be paid are, it is true, all laid down by the Home Secretary, either in the Police Regulations or in pursuance of powers granted him by those regulations, but he himself has no authority to pay the men. This must be done from the local police fund which each police authority must maintain. Apart from grants-in-aid from the Exchequer, the sources of income of a police fund outside the Metropolitan police district are (1) the local authority, which is bound to allocate an amount from the rates sufficient to pay all the police expenses of their district after taking into account money received from other sources, and (2) miscellaneous receipts of comparatively small amount. The police authority must then see that the force has somewhere to work, and somewhere to live unless it chooses to pay rent allowances instead of providing houses. It must also provide premises in which persons taken into custody by the police may be temporarily confined. The Home Secretary has no power to build or repair a police station or a police house if the local police authority fails in its duty. The police authority has other miscellaneous but important functions. It must supply the men with uniform and equipment and pay them pensions when they are injured or retire, and allowances if they perform special duties. It must appoint a Chief Officer to command the force; at least the law requires it to do so in the case of a county force, and in practice it is necessary to do so in a borough force. All these things and many others must, and can only, be done by the local police authority which is responsible for the force.

Further light may be thrown on the activities of provincial police authorities if they are considered in relation first to Chief Constables, and then to local authorities, i.e. county and borough councils.

Police Authorities and Chief Constables

The distribution of functions and the relations between police authorities and Chief Constables vary much according to the personalities involved: at one extreme one will find the Chief Constable who 'runs' his police authority; at the other extreme the

Chief Constable who is hamstrung by them. But this much can be said: a Chief Constable in a county has normally a much freer hand than a Chief Constable in a borough. This is partly due to the fact that a Standing Joint Committee does not usually meet more often than once every three months, whereas a Watch Committee usually meets once a month. This is a matter of practice: except in the case of one or two combined police authorities there is no statutory requirement on the matter. Moreover, a Chief Constable in a town is much more under the eyes of the members of his police authority than he is in a county where he may live far from them. More important still is the difference in statutory powers. In a county it is the Chief Constable who appoints men to the force, promotes them (or not), and takes disciplinary measures against them when necessary, even to the extent of dismissal. The Standing Joint Committee will probably consider that it has a general duty to see that the Chief Constable is exercising these powers in a reasonable way, but it has no right to interfere with his actions in these matters, and an aggrieved member of the force has no right of appeal to the police authority who will, except in very exceptional cases, refuse to consider his complaint. In a borough, on the other hand, the power to appoint, promote and take disciplinary action against members of the force is vested in the Watch Committee. Normally it delegates these duties to the Chief Constable, but his decisions have to be submitted to the Watch Committee for ratification and it will sometimes have an opinion of its own, particularly on matters of promotion and discipline.

Differences between police authorities and Chief Constables arise most commonly over the expenditure of money. The Chief Constable's natural desire is to enlarge his force, and to see it provided with more and better equipment. The police authority, on the other hand, will equally naturally also be thinking of the rates; and its duty to the ratepayers, as well as the Home Office's duty to the taxpayers, are perhaps not always properly appreciated by the Chief Constable who will be thinking how well the district could be policed if he had some more men and equipment.

Other sources of difficulty, but only in the boroughs, are promotions and discipline. The Chief Constable may suspect members of the Watch Committee of promoting their friends, and of being lax or corrupt in their administration of the discipline code. Sometimes politics are involved. There have been cases of Labour councils objecting to the part played by the police during industrial troubles. In counties it is less usual to find a divergence between the politics of the police authority and Chief Constable. Where the Chief Constable is on good terms with the leading members of the police authority, tells them what he is doing, discusses with them plans for the future, and receives advice and support from the authority on the matters with which they are properly concerned, the partnership is seen at its best. Where the Chief Constable does not take the police authority into his confidence, rides roughshod over their wishes, and the members of the committee interfere with everything they can, intrigue against him and frustrate him at every turn, the 'partnership' is seen at its worst.

The best example of difficulties of this sort is to be found in the events at St. Helens which culminated in 1928 in an enquiry under the Tribunals of Enquiry (Evidence) Act, 1921. Friction first arose in 1918 when the police were concerned with the conduct of a club in which a member of the Watch Committee was interested. A few years later one of the aldermen was charged with intimidation and convicted. The police then brought proceedings against him for perjury. Next the Watch Committee tried to interfere with the disposition of particular policemen. Finally, in 1926, police were drafted from Liverpool to help the St. Helens force with industrial troubles. The committee objected to the way in which the Liverpool men exercised their powers and thought it should determine where they should be placed. Meetings of the committee became disorderly; members rose to strike one another; there was confusion and chaos at discipline cases. The committee complained of the way the Chief Constable dealt with them, of his conduct before the magistrates, of his dealings with members of the force and Federation, and of his behaviour to the public, and alleged that he used the police for his private purposes. Events culminated in the Watch Committee dismissing the Chief Constable: he appealed to the Home Secretary under the Police (Appeals) Act, 1927, and was reinstated. The Tribunal which was set up under the Act of 1921 reported that the Chief Constable had probably had a very free hand from 1905, when he took over the force, until 1923 when, largely instigated by an alderman who was hostile to him on personal grounds, a section of the committee withdrew their support from him and began looking more thoroughly into police matters. The Tribunal considered that the Chief Constable, though a severe disciplinarian, had done nothing which should have forfeited the confidence of the committee. In conclusion, the Tribunal expressed its doubts whether the Chief Constable of a borough council should be at the mercy of a temporary majority of a Watch Committee acting perhaps on party lines, either in reference to breaches of discipline in the force, or in regard to his own tenure of office.

These events at St. Helens are, of course, not typical, but they are of interest as showing what can happen in an extreme case. Moreover, it is more difficult to find out about the system when it is running well than when it is running badly.

There has not been enough experience of combined police authorities to see whether their relations with Chief Constables will develop on any special lines. It may be that being hybrids, *ad hoc* bodies with no tradition behind them, they will find themselves in a weak position *vis-à-vis* their Chief Constables. All one can say at present is that where the scheme is a county scheme and the police authority has the powers of a Standing Joint Committee, its relations with the Chief Constable will probably develop on the usual lines found in counties, and where the scheme is a borough scheme and the police authority has the powers of a Watch Committee, relations will develop on the usual lines found in boroughs, but there may be features of both kinds of relations in both types of scheme.

Police Authorities and Local Authorities

A police authority has relations not only with the Home Office and with its Chief Constable, but also with what may be described as the parent local authority or authorities.

A Standing Joint Committee is not a committee of the county council, but a joint committee of county councillors and justices. It is not subject to the control of the county council or of the justices in Quarter Sessions. The Standing Joint Committee indents on the county council for the funds it requires for police purposes and the county council is bound to comply with these demands. The police service is in this respect in an exceptional position: in other spheres, the county finance committee and the council usually have more control. It is sometimes suggested that Standing Joint

Committees should be required to furnish to county councils for their information or approval their estimates of expenditure on the police. The present position is certainly anomalous in some ways, chiefly in that it gives justices, who are appointed, not elected, power to spend other people's money without having to think how they are going to levy it and without having to defend the rates before the local electors. Nor is there now, as there used to be, any statutory limit to the rate which may be levied for police purposes. But there is in fact little evidence that Standing Joint Committees are extravagant, and there might well be difficulties if one gave the county council control over the expenditure of a body which was not a committee of the council. The theoretical objections to the present arrangement are probably lessened by the fact that the financial officer of the county council is also the financial officer of the Standing Joint Committee. The problem would, of course, no longer arise if the control of the police in counties were transferred to county councils. It is understandable that county councillors on occasion feel that they should at least discuss matters of police administration. Sometimes, though rarely, they succeed, as recently in Buckinghamshire, where the county council took an interest in an argument which was going on between the Standing Joint Committee and the Home Secretary about using policemen to clean police stations. Nor do the justices in Quarter Sessions have any control over Standing Joint Committees, though sometimes the committee will send them a report on police matters simply for their information.

Difficulties between the county council and the Standing Joint Committee sometimes arise because the committee is responsible not only for buildings used by the police, but also for county property of a judicial character—that is, accommodation for Quarter Sessions, justices out of session and clerks to justices. The County Councils Association has criticised this arrangement as anomalous, involving as it does in many cases the absence of county council control over county halls, used, as the great majority are, partly for the administration of justice.

A Watch Committee, on the other hand, is, as we have seen, a committee of the town council: the police fund in a borough is a branch of the general rate fund and the council has therefore some voice in police matters. Exactly how much is not always agreed, but the current view seems to be that the council can concern itself with anything which involves the expenditure of money, but not with other matters. The Municipal Corporations Act, 1882, requires the council to approve the expenditure of the Watch Committee, and instances of councils refusing to approve expenditure proposed by Watch Committees have often occurred, but the system is not altogether satisfactory because the council often lacks full information about the matter at issue.

Decisions of the Watch Committee which do not involve the expenditure of money often come before the council for information, but any attempt to discuss them is ruled out of order. Members of councils make spasmodic attempts to get round these restrictions, usually in connection with promotions or in order to question the general efficiency of the Chief Constable. In one instance recently, where the Council was dissatisfied with some promotions made by the Watch Committee, on being informed by the Town Clerk that they could only discuss matters involving police expenditure, the council refused to approve the Watch Committee's financial proposals. Later a town councillor proposed that the council should constitute itself as the Watch Committee, but this clearly would have been an infringement of the Municipal Corporations Act, 1882, which requires the council to appoint a Watch Committee.

In another case recently the council claimed that it and not the Watch Committee should be responsible for the appointment of the Chief Constable. In spite of opposition from the Watch Committee, the council actually interviewed the candidates and recommended the Watch Committee to appoint one of them. The Watch Committee complied with the council's request and the Home Secretary approved the appointment, but the Home Office informed the council that the procedure adopted was open to considerable objection 'having regard to the direct responsibility of the Watch Committee for the appointment of members of a police force'. It seems clear that if councils were to make a practice of interfering with police matters other than those involving money, Watch Committees would be weakened and hampered in the exercise of their powers and responsibilities. No one would pretend that Watch Committees are perfect, but the safeguards of election from time to time by the council and the conduct of most affairs in public, together with the control exercised by the Home Office, should be adequate; and having appointed persons to establish and maintain a police force, it is desirable that the council should make them feel, and indeed that they should be, really responsible for doing their task.

In the case of combined police authorities, the councils of the participating authorities have no control over the expenditure incurred by the combined authority except what they can exercise through their representatives on the combined authority. The county councils and the borough councils concerned are simply required to contribute the sum required by the combined police authority in certain proportions which are laid down in the scheme under which the combined police authority is constituted. This deprives the borough councils concerned of the control over police expenditure which they previously possessed. It does not, of course, affect county councils who never had any such control.

Assistance from Local Authority Officials

A police authority obviously needs an official (indeed several) to look after its business—not only to summon it, prepare the agenda for meetings, write the minutes, but to do all the things which are required by statute or regulation to be done by the police authority, such as to pay the force wages, allowances, and pensions on retirement. The official who is, as it were, secretary to the authority is known as the Clerk to the Police Authority. In boroughs the Town Clerk, who is by custom normally secretary to all committees of the council, is always Clerk to the Watch Committee. In counties the Clerk of the County Council is *ex officio* Clerk to the Standing Joint Committee. This is laid down in the Local Government (Clerks) Act, 1931. The Clerk of the County Council is also practically always Clerk of the Peace. Having the same man in these various posts probably makes for smooth working of the machine. In the case of combined police authorities, the schemes require the authority to appoint a clerk, leaving them free to choose whom they wish. Normally the clerk of the largest participating authority has been appointed.

Considerable assistance is also given by local authorities' treasurers, who manage the police funds, and by their surveyors, architects and other technical experts who help with police buildings. The division of duties between the local authority's staff and the Chief Constable varies considerably. In some places the local authority's officials do all the work connected with paying the force, calculating pensions, ordering equipment, etc.; in others the work is done in the Chief Constable's office, often with the assistance of some local authority staff.

Another important field in which the local authority's staff assist the police is in connection with prosecutions. In the great majority of cases in which the police prosecute they are not legally represented. Where they are legally represented, this may be by a member of the staff of the Clerk of the Peace or of the Town Clerk, or by a private solicitor. In some areas the conditions of appointment of the Chief Constable require him to consult the Clerk of the Peace or Town Clerk in certain classes of case, and to use their staff and not a private solicitor for prosecutions which are not conducted by the police. In other areas the Chief Constable can do as he likes.

The present arrangements regarding police prosecutions do not work satisfactorily in all areas. In some, Chief Constables do not ask for legal representation by the local authority's staff as often as they ought, and leave the case in the hands of a police officer, partly it would appear because they are not satisfied with the quality of the assistance given to them in the past by the local authority's legal staff, partly for reasons of prestige. In other areas, where the Chief Constable is obliged to consult the Clerk of the Peace or Town Clerk, differences of opinion sometimes arise and are not always easy to settle. Other unsatisfactory practices which occasionally occur are for an officer of the local authority to be employed where the authority are also concerned with the defence, e.g. in a prosecution against the driver of one of their vehicles, or where the Clerk to the Police Authority acts as Clerk of the Court, e.g. at Quarter Sessions. The representatives of the local authorities have recently expressed themselves rather uncompromisingly against giving Chief Constables a free hand in this matter. They appear to think the present arrangements work satisfactorily, and that if they are to be altered, this should be in the direction of giving more influence to the Clerk to the Police Authority. It would seem that no rule of general application should be laid down in this matter, where so much depends on the characters and qualifications of the persons involved.

Control of the Police by the Justices

This is a complicated question which cannot be fully treated here, but a few words must be said about it in order to complete the picture of the various agencies which exercise some control over the police.

For many centuries, as we have seen, justice and constable were the superior and inferior conservators of the peace, and while the constable was sometimes given orders by other persons, he came mainly under the control of the justices. Looked at from another point of view, it may be said that the magistrates were to some extent police officers as well as magistrates: for instance, they not only issued the warrant of arrest, but saw to the necessary enquiries by their constables, examined the prisoner, and committed him for trial. In 1829, the policeman was separated from the magistrate in the Metropolitan police district. The Commissioners of Police who were to appoint the constables and organise the force were, it is true, to be sworn in as justices of the peace, but they were not to do the ordinary court work of justices. The Metropolitan magistrates lost virtually all their powers over the police, and what may be described as their executive police functions, e.g. examining prisoners, which were transferred to the new police office, and they have never regained them.

The position in the City of London is in this respect identical to that in the Metropolitan police district. The Commissioner appoints the constables and has done so since 1839, and they are to obey 'all such lawful commands as they may from time to time receive from the Commissioner'—not from the justices. Nor can the justices suspend or dismiss the constables: the Commissioner alone can do this.

In the boroughs outside London, the justices lost their power to appoint constables in 1835 when this power was transferred to the Watch Committees of the reformed corporations. It was, however, provided that the constables were to obey such lawful commands as they might from time to time receive from any of the justices of the peace having jurisdiction in the borough or in any county in which they were called upon to act 'for conducting themselves in the execution of their office'. It is not clear what exactly was meant by this, but it seems evident that the powers of the justices over the police were substantially reduced in 1835, faced as the justices then were with the rival of a Watch Committee which had power to make regulations for preventing neglect or abuse or for rendering the constables efficient in the discharge of their duties. The justices were, it is true, given power to suspend or dismiss any constable whom they thought negligent, but this power was also given to Watch Committees.

The position in boroughs was slightly altered in 1882, and it now is that a constable must obey all such lawful commands as he receives from any justice having jurisdiction in the borough or in any county in which the constable is called upon to act. The power of any two justices to dismiss a negligent constable was repealed in 1882, and the power to suspend him from duty has fallen almost wholly into abeyance, specially since 1920 when the Police Regulations prescribed a discipline code and in great detail the procedure to be followed by Chief Constables and Watch Committees in disciplinary cases.

In the counties, the justices remained responsible for the administration of the police until 1888, and when in that year administrative control over the county police was given to joint committees of justices and county councillors, the functions of the justices as conservators of the peace were safeguarded. It was laid down in the Local Government Act, 1888, that 'nothing in this Act shall affect the powers, duties and liabilities of justices of the peace as conservators of the peace, or the obligation of the Chief Constable or other constables to obey their lawful orders given in that behalf'.

Exactly what these powers amount to in counties and boroughs is not altogether clear. The statutes do not specifically give the justices power to give orders to the police: all they say is that the police must obey 'lawful orders' given by the justices. In any event, whatever powers the justices have in this regard, they are in fact seldom exercised. Virtually the only type of occasion in which they interest themselves in the operations of the police is in times of civil disturbance, and even then it is unlikely that they would function as a body. The Chief Constable at a time of crisis would be in close touch with the chairman of the police authority and in boroughs also with the mayor who is *ex officio* a magistrate (and often Chairman of the Police Authority), but it is very rare for the justices as a body to give the Chief Constable or any other police officer specific orders. The position is admittedly strange: there is no statutory provision enabling the police authority to give the police orders, but in practice their control over the police is far closer than the justices'. While the magistrates plainly have a responsibility for maintaining the peace by virtue of their Commission from the Crown, it is equally plain that their powers have become rather shadowy.

Besides the authority over the police which the justices possess as conservators of the peace, they may in counties also require them to perform extra duties connected with the police. Similar powers are possessed in counties by Standing Joint Committees and county councils, and in boroughs by Watch Committees. Police authorities make use of their powers by requiring the police to perform duties under, for example, the Diseases of Animals Acts and the Weights and Measures Acts, but it would appear that the justices have for many years not exercised their powers in this regard. It is also rare for justices to exercise their powers over special constables, i.e. to make regulations for their guidance or to remove them for misconduct or neglect of duty: special constables normally get their orders from the Chief Constable.

Complaints against the Police

Among the important matters which are settled locally and not centrally are complaints against the police. If a member of the public has a complaint to make against a police officer, he should address himself to the disciplinary authority, that is, in a county to the Chief Constable and in a borough to the Watch Committee, though in either case the complaint will probably be investigated by the Chief Constable or his staff. If he writes to the Home Office, he will usually be told that the Home Secretary can take no action in the matter, and that he should make his complaint to the authority in whom disciplinary control of the force is vested. In some cases the Home Secretary will, before replying, enquire into the matter, that is, call for a report from the Chief Constable, but it is rare for him to take any further action. It is probable that if there were constant complaints about a particular force, H.M. Inspector would be asked to investigate the administration of discipline in that force and advise the Chief Constable to take appropriate action, and in the last resort grant might be withheld on the ground that the force was not efficiently and properly administered. But the Home Secretary seldom interferes with an individual case: for instance he would rarely, if ever, suggest that compensation should be paid to a complainant even if he thought this justifiable. An aggrieved person would be left to press his case as best he could, if necessary by bringing an action against the officer concerned.

Some complaints which are made against the police are groundless: there is, for instance, a certain class of neurotics who suffer from delusions that the police are persecuting them in some way or other. Other complaints are exaggerated, but to some extent justified. Others are wholly justified. But into whichever class a complaint falls, it is extremely important that it should be fully and impartially investigated. It is doubtful whether this always happens under the present system, for a Chief Constable or police authority when investigating a complaint is sometimes too anxious to defend the reputation of the force and whitewash individual police officers. There is, of course, the safeguard of the courts, but few people have the means or knowledge to embark on legal proceedings. Many complainants would no doubt feel that they had received greater justice if their complaints were investigated by the Home Office, and the Chief Constable or police authority instructed to make suitable amends; but this would, of course, be a dangerous innovation, as it would mean that the Home Secretary was interfering with the executive actions of the police and in practice deciding issues normally left to the law courts. Such action would be particularly open to objection where the complaint had a political flavour. It is not easy, therefore, to see what the ideal arrangement would be.

There is another major question which is not adequately covered in the existing law or practice, namely, the procedure for dealing with complaints against Chief Constables. During recent years, allegations, some of them serious, have been made against several Chief Constables. Irregularities of one kind and another have been alleged concerning, e.g. petrol, the use of policemen as 'batmen', and the arbitrary administration of discipline. Some of these allegations have been made by members of the force; others by members of the public; yet others by H.M. Inspectors. It is obviously extremely important that whenever a *prima facie* case has been made out, the complaints should be fully and fairly investigated. In some cases the police authority has held an enquiry into such complaints as appeared worthy of notice, settling the procedure *ad hoc;* in others, where the allegations were in the nature of a general reflection on the Chief Constable's administration of the force, the Home Secretary has appointed an independent committee of enquiry. An enquiry by a police authority suffers from the inherent disadvantage that the Chief Constable must of necessity have been closely associated with members of the authority and may have personal friends or enemies on it. On the other hand, the report of an enquiry by an independent tribunal appointed by the Home Secretary is not binding on the police authority by whom any disciplinary action must be taken (there have been instances of the authority refusing to accept the tribunal's findings). The present position is unsatisfactory in other respects too, and it is to be hoped that some method will be found of improving it. Some recommendations on the matter have been made by the Oaksey Committee.

An official such as a Chief Constable who is responsible to a committee is often much less closely supervised than an official who is responsible to a superior officer. It is difficult for members of committees to discover exactly what and how much their officers are doing, as they must inevitably rely mainly on such information as the officers supply them with. But if the system is to function efficiently, there must be means for discovering and remedying slackness, weaknesses and abuses.

Reform of Police Authorities

Very few people in England to-day recommend taking the provincial police out of the hands of local police authorities, but many advocate certain reforms in the constitution and functions of these authorities. The most important of these are the transfer of the control of the police in counties to county councils, and the substitution of the Chief Constable for the Watch Committee as the appointing, promoting, and disciplinary authority in boroughs.

(i) Standing Joint Committees

When county councils were established in 1888, the question whether they could safely be entrusted with the control of the police was much discussed in the House of Commons. The Government defended its proposal of joint committees of councillors and magistrates on the following lines: conditions in town and county were very different; the inhabitants of boroughs had become accustomed to municipal government for many years; they were educated in the science of government to a degree which it would take the inhabitants of counties some years to attain; the county magistrates had managed the police with perfect prudence and judgment and great economy; the Government was far from implying distrust of an elected body that had the confidence of the people; nor would it object if that body was swayed by a general sympathy with the people, but great gusts of popular feeling which arose when a particular law became unpopular represented only the 'passion' of the moment, not the 'true feeling' of the country; a body of men dependent for election on the sympathy of the masses might be less able to resist that feeling than magistrates.

Few voices were raised in support of the Government's proposal. It was thought to be a dangerous compromise, and that one should not run risks of paralysis in a body dealing with the police. It would lead to friction between Quarter Sessions and county councils. Many members pressed that control of the police should remain with the magistrates, not always on the ground advanced by one speaker that if control of the police were taken from the magistrates 'and their sons', people would be less anxious to become magistrates. A minority spoke in favour of county councils. Too many powers were being left with the justices who were not always impartial and not in sympathy with the people. Control by the elected representatives of the people would foster that sympathy between the police and the public which was desirable. There was no reason to fear that county councils would not support the Chief Constable in times of trouble; public order would in fact be better promoted than if the police were left in the hands of the magistrates who were preoccupied in adhering to 'the glories of the past'. The justices in counties had often been in conflict with the Chief Constable whereas in boroughs there was greater harmony. Only one member suggested that the Home Office should assume control, but this was turned down as 'a most monstrous doctrine'.

Throughout these arguments, it seems to have been assumed that the chief duty of those who controlled the police was to supervise how they enforced the law and what action they took during civil disturbances. This led to advocacy of control by a judicial body. But even by 1888 a great deal of the work of the authority in charge of the police was concerned with what are usually known as administrative matters, namely, pay, clothing, conditions of service, buildings, etc. Only one member seems to have realised this when he recommended that administrative and judicial bodies should be separated, and that county councils were more suited than justices to administrative functions such as appointing Chief Constables.

The Government in 1888 appear to have had it in mind that Standing Joint Committees might only be a temporary arrangement and that if the county councils proved themselves worthy of the responsibility, they might later be given control of the police. By 1914, when county councils had been entrusted with new and important powers on many occasions, the Government of the day thought it safe to give them control over the police, but the Bill which it prepared to abolish Standing Joint Committees never reached the Statute Book. It appears to have been forgotten by 1919, for when the organisation of the police was reviewed in that year from most angles by the Desborough Committee, no one appears to have suggested taking control of the police from Standing Joint Committees. Indeed the Home Office witness recommended that Watch Committees should be composed half of town councillors and half of magistrates, on the rather curious ground that if the Government was to assume greater control of borough forces and give them greater financial aid, the body governing the police should contain representatives of the Crown; moreover, from the purely practical point of view, he added, this would give greater stability to the police authority. The Desborough Committee did not adopt this suggestion; nor did it recommend the abolition of Standing Joint Committees. The Home Office witness before the Royal Commission on Local Government (1923) said the Home Office were not aware of any necessity for a change, and indeed there were palpable objections to removing the justices' responsibility for the police. He did not specify what these objections were, but merely said that having regard to the position the justices still held as conservators of the peace and the historical ground for the arrangement, it seemed a sound one. There has been no pressure from county Chief Constables to alter the constitution of their police authorities; they are probably apprehensive that their life would be less easy if for the justices, who in many places do not take a very lively interest in police affairs, there were substituted county councillors.

Recently the matter came to the fore because the Home Secretary, Mr. Chuter Ede, was in favour of transferring control of the police to county councils. He was himself a member of a county council and of a Standing Joint Committee for many years, and this experience led him to think the present arrangement 'entirely archaic'. He has pointed out that some Standing Joint Committees report to the county council and to Quarter Sessions, and that some do not, but that the Standing Joint Committee's report cannot even be adopted by the council—all the council can do is to thank the committee for telling them what they have done with the council's money. As yet, however, Mr. Ede has not introduced legislation to make the change.

It is undoubtedly difficult to justify to-day on theoretical or other grounds the constitution of Standing Joint Committees. It now seems certain that there are men on the councils who are properly fitted by their past experience to deal with such a matter as the police, which was doubted by the Attorney General in 1888, and it is now generally accepted that the control over the expenditure of money should be vested in those who have to raise it and in the elected representatives of those who have to provide it. No Government now would dare to suggest that it wished to retain magistrates on police authorities because it regarded them as its representatives and could trust them to look after its interests.

(ii) *Watch Committees*

Few people recommend changes in the constitution of Watch Committees (apart from the question of the area for which they should be responsible), but a certain curtailment of their powers has been advocated at intervals almost ever since they were first set up in 1835. More recently the Desborough Committee recommended that the power of appointment and promotion and disciplinary powers in borough forces should be vested in the Chief Constable. This is what the Committee said about discipline:

'We consider that the divided authority which results from a constable being under the orders of the Chief Constable but subject to the Watch Committee for purposes of discipline is very undesirable, and we are strongly of opinion that the public discussion of the delinquencies of individual constables before the Watch Committee or the Town Council is prejudicial to discipline. If such matters are dealt with by an elected Committee there is a risk of members of the Committee being canvassed by or on behalf of the constable concerned or their being influenced by personal matters which have arisen between themselves and the police. Though the risk of irregularities will be greater in the small boroughs than in the large city forces, the principal objections are inherent in the system, and we recommend that, subject to what we say below with regard to a right of appeal against dismissal, disciplinary authority over all lower ranks should be vested in the Chief Constables in the borough forces in England and Wales.' Similar considerations prompted the Committee's recommendations regarding appointment and promotion.

From time to time since the Desborough report, unfavourable comments have been made on the way in which Watch Committees administered discipline. 'No amount of Regulations will make some members of Watch Committees decide disciplinary matters in a proper judicial spirit', wrote one of the Inspectors in 1920; and the same thought must have passed through the mind of many an Inspector since then. Mr. Herbert Morrison, who had experience of the London County Council's administration of semi-disciplinary business, said, when Home Secretary, that even where there is a very good machine, with a good legal department, very good advisers and a long tradition in handling such things, it is a strain to keep a committee straight in handling delicate quasi-judicial matters.

On the other hand, the Police Federation has for many years been in favour of the present system and wishes to see it extended to counties. The matter has been somewhat confused by the fact that where the Watch Committee has delegated its disciplinary powers to the Chief Constable, and rehears the case before confirming the Chief Constable's decision, the police officer appears to have, and indeed may properly be said to have, a right of appeal against the Chief Constable. This procedure is contrasted with that in counties where the Chief Constable has the last word, subject to appeal in most cases to the Home Secretary. The democratic procedure in boroughs is contrasted with the 'quasi-military' methods used by Chief Constables in counties. The Federation does not have the same confidence in Chief Constables as the Inspector of Constabulary who, in evidence before the Desborough Committee in 1919, said that 'the majority of Chief Constables have been appointed from a class in life which makes it unlikely that personal matters are likely to intervene' in their administration of discipline. He added that as Chief Constables had generally served in the navy or army, they had learned to regard the care of their men as their first duty and were quite capable of giving every man a fair trial. The Federation's case has been pressed in particular in connection with amalgamations, in order to 'safeguard' the position of the borough man, but the Government has always resisted attempts to give combined police authorities the powers of Watch Committees either over all members of the combined force or over such members of it as were previously in borough forces. There is less substance in the Federation's case now that the police have a right of appeal against reductions in pay or rank, as well as against dismissal or enforced resignation, and the weight of evidence seems to indicate that a committee is not a good disciplinary body whether looked at from the interests of the men or the interests of discipline. With the abolition of the smaller borough forces in 1947, the reform is less urgently needed than it was in 1920, but it would still seem desirable to make it; and it has now been recommended by the Oaksey Committee.

Any attempt to alter the present arrangement would no doubt be criticised as yet another encroachment on the powers of local authorities, but it should be observed that they would be losing their powers not to a Government Department, but to the Chief Constable whom they appoint.

CHAPTER VI

The Metropolitan Police Force

Distinctive Characteristics

IT is paradoxical that the force which is most familiar to foreign observers and which is usually regarded as the prototype of all British police forces should be the only one in the whole country which does not exemplify one of the most characteristic features of the British police service—its control by local authorities. British and foreign writers make much of the local control of the British police; they refer to the 'constitutional principle' that the preservation of law and order is in Great Britain primarily the function of local authorities. How is this principle reconciled with the fact that one in four of our policemen belongs to a force over which no local authority has any control whatsoever and which is under the direct control of the Home Secretary? In truth the Metropolitan police force confounds the theories of most writers about police organisation in this country. No local authority plays any part in its management, and yet it is popular and usually considered to be scrupulous in the exercise of its powers. A recent Home Secretary described it as the most popular force in the whole country, indeed in the civilised world; and yet, he said, it is a State police, a national force. It would, however, be wrong to think of the force as having always been popular: it has been severely criticised at intervals ever since 1829 and has been the subject of many official enquiries.

The Metropolitan police force differs in many ways from all other forces in this country. In the first place it is far larger: in 1949 the authorised establishment of the force was 20,000. The actual strength was only 15,500, but even so it was seven times the size of the next largest and 700 times the size of the smallest force. The area of which it is in charge, the Metropolitan police district, extends for about 15 miles from Charing Cross in all directions, except for the City of London which has its own force.

Secondly, the Metropolitan police district cuts across ordinary local government boundaries: it includes the whole of the counties of London and Middlesex, parts of the counties of Kent, Surrey, Essex and Hertford, and the three county boroughs of Croydon, West Ham and East Ham; but none of the councils of these counties or county boroughs has any voice whatsoever in the administration or control of the Metropolitan police force although they have to pay towards its cost. Thirdly, for the Metropolitan police force, the Home Secretary is the police authority, that is to say, he has *vis-à-vis* this force the powers and functions possessed by provincial police authorities *vis-à-vis* their forces, but the relationship in practice is very different. He also has over the Metropolitan police force the powers he possesses *qua* Home Secretary over provincial forces: for instance, the regulations he makes under the Police Act, 1919, apply to the Metropolitan police force in the same way as they apply to any other force. In the Metropolitan police district, therefore, the Home Secretary combines the functions of central and local police authority. To the Home Secretary, as central authority, the Metropolitan police force is only one of the 129 forces of England and Wales, though far the largest and most important: in dealing with matters affecting the police service as a whole he has to consider and take account of the circumstances and requirements of all forces, Metropolitan, county, borough, and combined; but as the police authority for the Metropolitan police district, he is in theory at any rate personally and directly responsible for the administration and policy of the force.

The Senior Officers

The Chief Officer of the force is the Commissioner of Police of the Metropolis. He is assisted by five Assistant Commissioners, one of whom is appointed Deputy Commissioner. The Commissioner and the Assistant Commissioners are appointed by the Crown, on the recommendation of the Home Secretary. As we have seen, they do not hold the office of constable, but are justices of the peace, an arrangement which would appear to be now rather anomalous. The next in rank are Commanders; then come Deputy Commanders, and after that the ranks are the same as outside London, descending from Chief Superintendent to Constable. The Commissioner appoints all members of the force, though in an organisation of this size the power of appointment is, of course, delegated to his subordinates. The power of promotion is also the Commissioner's, but promotions to the higher ranks and appointments from outside the force to these ranks are subject to the Home Secretary's approval. The Commissioner is the disciplinary authority, just as the Chief Constable is in a county force, and it is therefore the Commissioner who punishes, suspends and dismisses members of the force, subject to their right of appeal to the Home Secretary, *qua* central authority, not *qua* police authority, under the Police (Appeals) Acts.

It is difficult to delineate in a few words the respective spheres of the Home Secretary and Commissioner which in any event vary from time to time according to the personalities concerned. Broadly speaking it may be said that the Home Secretary is responsible for general policy, and the Commissioner for the detailed management of the force, but the Home Secretary can give the Commissioner instructions on any matter however detailed or technical. In practice, however, he will normally confine himself to laying down general principles and will leave the Commissioner to apply them to individual cases, and he will not concern himself with the technicalities of police work unless complaints have been made. For the Home Secretary is particularly concerned with matters affecting the relations between the police and the public, and has often been in the position of protecting the public from the over-zealous police. Besides being ultimately responsible for the executive actions of the force, the Home Secretary is also responsible for what may be called its administration: he decides, for instance at what ages the various ranks shall be required to retire; how many medical officers there shall be; he awards pensions; and lays down general regulations regarding sick leave and many other matters.

The Commissioner of Police of the Metropolis has certain powers which in the provinces are possessed not by the police or the police authority, but by the local authority or the justices. For instance, the police in London license and supervise public carriages, including taxi-cabs; they regulate street collections; they deal with applications to permit the sale of intoxicating liquor during prohibited hours on special occasions. It is true that provincial local authorities can often delegate to the police their powers in connection with these matters; but the position is different in London, though perhaps not quite as different as it appeared to Maitland, who wrote, in 1885, that London was subjected 'to a police regimen such as exists in no other part of England.'

Throughout the 120 years of its existence, the Metropolitan police force has not produced from its own ranks a Commissioner, or, with three exceptions, an Assistant Commissioner. Moreover, a fairly large proportion of those in the next senior ranks have at most times not been promoted from the force, but have been brought in from outside, not from provincial forces, but from other professions. There have been 14 Commissioners since 1829; all but four were previously members of the army or air force. Of the four who were not ex-servicemen, one was a barrister, and the other three were Civil Servants (two from the Indian Civil Service).

The practice of appointing Commissioners and other members of the higher ranks from outside the force has naturally been disheartening to many of its members, and has been criticised from time to time specially by the Police Federation. The question whether or not it was necessary must, of course, be a matter of opinion, but it would seem that the system of starting all men at the bottom and keeping them in the lower ranks for many years on the ordinary routine of police duty is not likely to produce men capable of filling the higher posts. Many of the abler men in the Metropolitan police gravitate to the C.I.D. where the work calls for special intelligence, but does not afford an all-round training in police administration. The Commissioner need not have expert knowledge of police matters, but he should be a man with a wide knowledge of men and affairs and administrative ability. A staff college was set up in 1933 in order to train members of the force for the higher posts, but it did not exist long enough substantially to alter the position: of the 113 men who went through the college, only one had by 1947 reached the rank of superintendent in the Metropolitan police force.

The experience of the last war, during which many young police officers rose to positions of considerable responsibility in the armed forces and in military government, showed that there was much latent capacity in the police of which full use was not then being made. If scope is given to police officers before they lose the energy of youth and become set in their ways, and if they are given some extra training of a liberalising kind, there seems no reason why the

Metropolitan police force should not produce its own Commissioner or, at any rate, most of the members of the higher ranks.

National and Imperial Services

The Metropolitan police force may also be distinguished from other forces in that it performs certain national and imperial functions. It maintains the Criminal Record Office, which is a national registry of crimes and of their perpetrators. 'C.R.O.', as it is known, contains, *inter alia*, a Central Finger Print Bureau for Great Britain. All police forces in Great Britain are required to send to New Scotland Yard the finger prints of all persons who have been convicted and sentenced to imprisonment for serious criminal offences, as specified in the statutory regulations on the subject. The records of C.R.O. are available for and are constantly used by provincial police forces. They are also available for foreign forces. C.R.O. issues as well as receives information as to crimes. The most important of its publications is the *Police Gazette*, which is issued daily and is supplied without charge to the police forces of Great Britain, Northern Ireland and certain imperial and foreign forces. It contains particulars of people wanted for crime, and of stolen property, etc.

Another way in which the Metropolitan police assist provincial forces is by lending them on request detective officers to help clear up particularly bad crimes, especially murders. This does not happen very often, on an average perhaps six times a year. No charge is made for this service, but the Metropolitan police require that they should be brought in from the start. The loaned detective remains under the control of the Commissioner, but he carries out his investigations in close co-operation with the local force and reports progress to the local Chief Constable. The Metropolitan police force is by no means the only force with a C.I.D.: most provincial forces have their own C.I.D. and even their own 'Special Branch', but the Special Branch of the C.I.D. at New Scotland Yard is in a sense the political police for the whole of the country. It aims at collecting information about 'undesirable' political persons and movements wherever their headquarters are situated; but Special Branch officers are not stationed outside the Metropolitan police district, except at a few ports where they work with the Home Office Immigration staff: elsewhere any necessary enquiries are made through the local force. The Metropolitan police force also performs more than local duties in connection with the protection of Royalty, Ministers of the Crown, and distinguished foreign visitors, and the extradition of persons surrendered to foreign countries.

For all these imperial and national services, the Metropolitan police force receives a contribution from the Exchequer of £100,000 a year. A grant for these services is authorised by the Police Act, 1909, but its amount is determined by the Home Secretary subject to the approval of the Treasury. The contribution has stood at this figure since 1909 when it was first introduced. If it was a reasonable figure then, it should be revised now, though it is no doubt difficult to make any exact estimate of the cost of the imperial and national services rendered by the Metropolitan police. The Exchequer also bears the cost of the Commissioner's salary, which is determined by the Home Secretary with the approval of the Treasury, and what was once the cost of one Assistant Commissioner (£1,200), but is now considerably less.

Finance

Apart from these special contributions from the Exchequer, the cost of the Metropolitan police is borne in equal shares by the rate-payer and the State as in the case of all other forces, but the arrangements for controlling expenditure are different. Peel saw the necessity for adequate control of Metropolitan police expenditure and property, if the new system was to be efficient and acceptable to the ratepayers, who were to have to pay for the police, but not to have any voice in its management. He decided that Home Office control should be reinforced by entrusting responsibility for all Metropolitan police property and for the administration of the Metropolitan police fund, out of which the expenses of the force were to be met, to someone who was not on the Commissioner's staff, the Receiver for the Metropolitan Police District. A provision to this effect was accordingly included in the Metropolitan Police Act, 1829.

The Receiver, like the Commissioner and Assistant Commissioners, is appointed by the Crown on the recommendation of the Home Secretary. There have been only six Receivers, including the present one, between 1829 and 1949, as contrasted with 15 Commissioners. The last four, including the present one, were Home

Office officials before appointment. Unlike the Commissioner, the Receiver seldom comes into the limelight; indeed few people know of the existence of the post, though it is important and constitutionally interesting.

The Receiver acts under the general directions of the Home Secretary; in fact he has been described as the Home Secretary's officer. He is this in a sense, namely, in that he is in effect appointed by the Home Secretary as are also the senior members of his staff, and in that he watches the Home Secretary's or, rather, the Exchequer's interests at New Scotland Yard. But he and his staff are not Home Office officials. Nor, on the other hand, are they part of the Commissioner's staff. The Receiver's salary is paid by the Exchequer; the salaries of his staff are paid from the Metropolitan police fund.

All proposals for new expenditure and all contracts have to be approved by the Home Secretary who settles any difference of opinion between the Commissioner and the Receiver on a financial matter. The Receiver also prepares an annual estimate of income and expenditure which requires the Home Secretary's approval and on which the Home Secretary decides the amount of the rate to be levied for police purposes in the Metropolitan police district. The Commissioner then issues rate warrants or precepts to the Metropolitan borough councils and to the rating authorities—county borough, urban or rural district councils—in the other parts of the Metropolitan police district. The demand is not for so many pounds of money, but for the levy of a rate of x shillings in the pound, the rate being the same for all parts of the Metropolitan police district. A full account of all moneys received and paid by the Receiver has to be made every year and laid before Parliament. These accounts are audited by the Controller and Auditor General, who reports thereon to the Public Accounts Committee of the House of Commons. The Home Secretary also has power to call for half-yearly or more frequent accounts.

Limits on the Home Secretary's Control

The Home Office is, through the Receiver, normally kept fairly fully informed on all the matters with which the Receiver is concerned, but it is not so easy for it to know what is going on in other spheres. There are various reasons for this. The most important

one is that the force is not inspected by H.M. Inspectors. There
were no such inspectors when the force was established in 1829,
and, when they were instituted in 1856, it was presumably felt that
it would be derogatory to the Home Secretary to require Crown
inspectors to consider whether the force for which he was directly
responsible was efficient. The result is that the Home Office often
knows less about the administration and activities of the Metropolitan police than it does about the administration and activities of
provincial forces. Then there is the fact that the Commissioner's
office is a large and complicated establishment, more like a Government department than the headquarters of other police forces in
Great Britain. Many matters have, of course, to be referred to the
Home Office for decision, e.g. any alteration in the establishment,
pensions, amendments to general orders to the force, but there is
probably a tendency for an organisation of this size to become
rather independent and for questions to be referred to the Home
Office in such a way that it is difficult for it not to agree to the
proposal made. Most Commissioners are in constant personal consultation with the Home Secretary, and indeed with the Permanent
Under Secretary of State at the Home Office, but the fact that the
Commissioner's salary is the same as the Permanent Under Secretary's is not without importance. Moreover, although Assistant
Commissioners are appointed by the Crown on the recommendation of the Home Secretary, the Commissioner has apparently at
most periods played a large part in their selection. It is, of course,
necessary that they should be acceptable to the Commissioner, but
in the appointment of Assistant Commissioners, the Home Secretary
should be more than a rubber stamp. There have recently been
signs that he has been playing a rather more positive rôle in the
making of these appointments.

Relations between the Home Office and the 'civil staff' at Scotland Yard are usually rather closer. These officials are not members
of the police force; nor are they Civil Servants, in that they are
distinct from the Civil Service of the Crown, though their duties
and conditions of service are very similar. They perform the duties
which in the case of provincial forces are performed by local
government officials or civilian employees on the Chief Constable's
staff or sometimes by police officers. The head of the civil staff is an
official of some standing known as the Secretary to the Metropolitan

Police, who corresponds in rank roughly to an Assistant Secretary in the Civil Service.

It may be suggested that inspection of the force by H.M. Inspectors would not be desirable as it would increase not only the Home Secretary's knowledge about the force, but also in effect his powers of control over it. Be this as it may, inspection would enable the Metropolitan police and provincial forces to benefit rather more than they do now from each other's experience. There is on some issues an unfortunate antagonism between them and a tendency to think that neither side has anything to learn from the other. Anything which can be done to break down this attitude would be advantageous and the single most useful step would be to arrange for H.M. Inspectors, if not formally to inspect, at least to be given facilities to survey certain aspects of the organisation and work of the force. Any change of this kind would, of course, need the most tactful handling, and even so would no doubt encounter much opposition, but it should in the long run be of considerable value to all forces.

Parliamentary Control

Parliament exercises rather closer supervision over the Metropolitan police force than it does over provincial forces. 'Government control means House of Commons control', said Mr. Moylan, the then Receiver, in his book on Scotland Yard in 1929. And he quoted the words of the Home Secretary (Sir W. Joynson-Hicks) in the debate on the Savidge case in 1928: 'I am the servant of the House of Commons, and every action I take, every decision I come to in regard to the police can be brought up and discussed here.' But these statements are really rather misleading: the House of Commons' control over the Metropolitan police is in fact slender. Take, for instance, the important matter of appointments. Many have been criticised in Parliament after they were announced, but none have been rescinded and there is little evidence that the Home Secretary has tried to meet these criticisms when making subsequent appointments. Even taking into account the part played by Whitehall in the selection of Chief Constables for local forces, it is clear that a local police authority exercises far more extensive powers in selecting their Chief Officer of police than does the House of Commons in the selection of the Commissioner and other senior officers of the

Metropolitan police force. Then there is the fact that the Chief Constable of a provincial force normally attends meetings of the police authority and can be questioned freely on any aspect of his work. It is true that the Home Secretary can be questioned in the House of Commons about any act of the Commissioner's or his subordinates, but the control the House can exercise by this method is less direct and rigorous than that exercised by a local police authority. Moreover, there is this difference between the two systems, that the House of Commons discusses most matters after they have happened, whereas local police authorities often determine future policy. To take only one example, local police authorities decide how many policemen are necessary in their area and then ask the Home Secretary to agree to it. In the case of the Metropolitan police force, the Home Secretary decides how many policemen should be employed in the light of the Commissioner's recommendation and this figure is not even reported to the House of Commons until after the event unless specially requested.

It is true that the House of Commons has the estimates of future expenditure from the Metropolitan police fund presented to it and that it can and often does debate these, but they are not really very detailed considering the large amounts involved ($£15\frac{1}{2}$ million for 1949–1950). Nor are the figures of actual expenditure which are given to Parliament much more detailed. In criticising these the Public Accounts Committee has the benefit of the views of the Controller and Auditor General, but examination by the Public Accounts Committee takes place usually several years after the event and has little influence on contemporary policy. Another factor which contributes towards making control by the House of Commons less searching than control by local police authorities is that Members of Parliament are rarely experts on police matters, whereas many members of Watch Committees and Standing Joint Committees acquire experience in administering a force over a period of years. The Commissioner makes an annual report to the Home Secretary which is presented to Parliament; this report contains a good deal of information about the administration of the force and about crime, but it is a rather formal document, and does not give information on which M.P.s could base legitimate criticisms.

Parliamentary control over the conduct of the police towards the public has, however, been rather more effective than its control over the administration of the force. There have been many occasions on which Parliament has expressed strong dissatisfaction with the methods of the Metropolitan police. The matter has not been relegated to a secret tribunal, but after being aired in Parliament has been enquired into by a Royal Commission or some other independent body.

Municipal Control

In 1829 there was no local authority with jurisdiction over the whole urban area of London, and, apart from the Corporation of the City of London, there was nothing in any part of London which we should recognise as municipal government. Even if there had been municipal bodies, it seems most improbable that Peel would have been willing to give them any control over the Metropolitan police, as he was convinced that the new police should be under one authority. They were therefore placed under the Home Office, although they were to be paid for almost wholly by the ratepayers of London. The Municipal Corporations Act, 1835, did not touch London and no alterations were made in the system of government of the Metropolis until 1855. Even then municipal boroughs were not created. The Metropolitan Board of Works was set up, but its powers lagged far behind those of the municipal authorities in many provincial cities. To have transferred the control of the police to this Board would have been a disastrous step from the point of view of the efficiency of the police, and it does not seem to have been suggested at the time.

It was not long, however, before a quite widespread demand arose that the Metropolitan police should be placed under local control; in fact the demand arose before competent local authorities existed in the London area. This may be thought curious. Part of the explanation appears to be that some of the pressure came from those who were opposed to the amalgamation of the City of London and Metropolitan police and who tried to strengthen their case with a general plea for municipal control of the police. Such statements as that 'local self-government was the most cherished right a Briton had' and that 'control of the Metropolitan police should *revert* to the municipalities' were made in Parliament in 1863 when the Government proposed to amalgamate the two forces. The other protagonists of local control were those who were critical of the conduct of the Metropolitan police at meetings and demonstrations, etc. During the second half of the last century there were many criticisms of the Metropolitan police for high-handedness and illegalities. The Commissioner was accused of pursuing a policy of 'military repression' in dealing with riots of the unemployed. These events gave grounds for saying that the police were out of touch with the people and should be controlled by their representatives. Local authority control was also advocated in the interests of economy. The establishment of the London County Council in 1888 gave further impetus to the movement and there was considerable support of the Council's claim to add the police to their other responsibilities; but Maitland's forecast of 1885, 'It seems improbable that the new corporation will be endowed with the powers of the Commissioner; he has become very necessary to us', proved correct. It is difficult to see how the London County Council could have taken over the police without breaking the Metropolitan police district into many pieces; for the council's area was then, as now, much smaller than the police area. Nevertheless, the disruption of the police district appears to have been contemplated with equanimity in quite responsible circles, e.g. a Select Committee of the House of Commons in 1867. Such a step would have been disastrous from the police point of view. Peel's boldness and imagination in making the Metropolitan police district as large as he did in 1829 are really remarkable, especially when one considers how small was the area assigned to the London County Council in 1888.

The early 20th century saw fewer demands for local authority control of the Metropolitan police, but they were still made, usually at times when the force had come in for some criticism. Thus it was suggested to the Royal Commission of 1908 which enquired into the way in which the Metropolitan police dealt with drunkenness, disorder and solicitation that the force should be put under the direct representatives of the electors as they would be more amenable to the wishes of the people than was the Home Secretary. The same suggestion was made in 1928 as a result of the Savidge case, but the House of Commons was easily persuaded by Sir W. Joynson-Hicks not to give up the 'democratic control' they possessed over the force. The London Labour Party had the municipalisation of the Metropolitan police on their programme for three elections, but the proposal aroused no interest amongst the electors and was dropped in about 1939.

Recently the demand has not been that the force should be controlled by the London County Council or other local authorities, but that the rating authorities should have some control over expenditure or, even more modestly, some information as to how the money they contribute is spent. Thus in 1938, it was suggested that a joint board representing the Home Office, Treasury, and local authorities should be set up to control expenditure on the force. The Home Secretary's answer was that responsibility for expenditure could not be divorced from responsibility for administration. In 1941 much the same reply was given when similar representations were made, but the Home Secretary, Mr. Morrison, hoped some machinery to meet the local authorities' desire for information might be set up after the war. In 1947 and 1948 they renewed their plea with the request that they should be given, for information only, copies of the estimates of police expenditure at an early date after their approval by Parliament, and that a small body representing the local authorities should be recognised as the medium for submitting questions relating to the administration and finances of the police and for discussing such questions with representatives of the force and the Home Office. But this request, too, has been rejected by the Home Secretary. In his view it would not be consistent with his responsibility to Parliament as police authority for the Metropolitan police district to recognise such a body. The local authorities' grievance is understandable and on the face of it their request seems reasonable and the grounds for refusing it rather odd. One would not have thought that supplying the local authorities with details of expenditure and discussing with them questions relating to the administration and finances of the force would detract from the Home Secretary's responsibility to Parliament. As matters stand the London ratepayer has to contribute a rate of 1s. 8d. in the £ towards the Metropolitan police, but has almost no means of controlling the expenditure of his money. He may be able to get a question asked in the House of Commons on some aspect of the administration of the force, but it is most unlikely that he will be able either to obtain sufficient information to be able to estimate whether the force is economically run or to bring sufficient pressure to bear to get any change made in the way the money is spent. He ought to be able to exercise some control through the Public Accounts Committee, but the difficulty is that the ratepayers have no organisation through which they can function in this matter, and in any case control through the Public Accounts Committee takes place long after the event.

Although it is seldom suggested now that the Metropolitan police force should be managed and controlled by the local authorities, it will be as well to review the arguments for and against such a step. Clearly the London County Council could not be substituted for the Home Secretary, as the county of London covers only about one-sixth of the Metropolitan police district. No one in their senses to-day would suggest breaking up the Metropolitan police force into a number of forces and putting each under the control of a local authority, viz. county and county borough authorities. If any change were to be made in the area for which the force is responsible, it should, from the purely technical point of view, be in the direction of enlarging it. It is certainly remarkable that apart from a few minor alterations which were made in 1946, it has not been found necessary to alter the area since 1840. It is sometimes suggested that if the Metropolitan police were under local authority control, they could not be entrusted with their present imperial and national functions, and that the Government would have either to provide a smaller police force of its own or to employ soldiers. It is true that in other countries it is rare, if not unknown, to find the protection of the capital left to the police of a local authority, and that except where the protection is given by the military, there is a police force under the direct control of the central government; but there are already many features of the British police system which are unique, and it is difficult to see why if the Metropolitan police were under local authority control, they could not be entrusted with the protection of the Sovereign, the Imperial Government, the Royal Palaces, the Houses of Parliament, and the maintenance of national criminal records and finger prints, etc. The local authority or authorities would no doubt ask for a special contribution from the Exchequer to cover these national services, but there do not seem to be any grounds for thinking that they would not recognise their importance and be willing to perform them. There might conceivably be difficulties if the Government and local police authority were of different political complexions: the police authority might, for instance, contrary to the Government's wishes, refuse to protect political demonstrators with whom they were not in sympathy; but provided the force maintained the peace reasonably well and in particular protected the King, members of the Government and the Houses of Parliament, etc., there seems no reason why the Government should maintain stricter control over events in the capital than elsewhere.

If one wished to do so, it would seem possible to devise a police authority suitable for the Metropolitan police district on the lines of the combined police authorities established under the Police Act, 1946. It would be composed of representatives of the local authorities, counties and county boroughs, whose area, or part of whose area, lay in the Metropolitan police district. The usual arguments against *ad hoc* authorities would apply to any such body and the scheme does not commend itself as practicable. But unless some concession is made to meet the local authorities' demands to play even a small part in the administration of the force, the Home Secretary may find himself faced with demands for a joint police authority for the Metropolitan police district on the lines of those that he has established in other areas. This would, however, not be such a satisfactory solution to the problem of London government as the opposite kind of process: namely, the abolition of the London County Council in favour of a Greater London Council, whose area would be not less and very likely greater than the Metropolitan police district, and which would be given control of the police.

Amalgamation with the City of London Force

Peel had hoped to include the City of London in the area for which the new force was to be responsible, but he was, in his own words, 'afraid to meddle' with the City. After recommendations for amalgamating the two areas for police purposes had been made by various parliamentary committees, a clause to this effect was included in the Metropolitan Police Bill of 1839, but it was dropped in face of terrific opposition. The Corporation remodelled its force on the lines of the Metropolitan police force with good results, but the case for merging the two still remained strong. In 1863 after the City police had failed to maintain a clear route for a royal procession and scenes of alarming confusion had ensued, the Government made another attempt to put the whole of London under one police authority. The case for amalgamation looked overwhelming, but the proposal met with the usual barrage of opposition: it was said, for instance, to threaten 'all free institutions and the middle classes'. The Government obtained leave to introduce a Bill, but it did not reach the Statute Book. In spite of the fact that amalgamation continued to be recommended at intervals by various bodies, including a Royal Commission, the Government did not make it a condition of financial assistance when this was first granted to the City in 1919. The Desborough Committee, though it heard some evidence, made no recommendation on the matter, and it has not in recent years been a live issue.

It is difficult for an outsider to form an opinion of value on the subject. He is naturally inclined to think the present arrangement anomalous and to suspect that amalgamation would lead to increased efficiency, especially in criminal investigation. He may also think that it would be possible for members of the Metropolitan police force if they were stationed in the City for long enough to acquire the special knowledge of conditions which are obviously essential to its efficient policing. But it may not be worth arousing opposition and causing difficulties by making a change which would, incidentally, still require an Act of Parliament. The arrangement has apparently not led to so serious a loss of efficiency as might have been expected, chiefly because the two forces have co-operated in their work. Moreover they function as one unit for wireless purposes and have recently set up a joint Company Fraud Department.

Conclusion

Whether or not we *call* the Metropolitan police force a state police, a national force, is immaterial. What is important is to try to estimate how far, as the law stands, it could be used by the central government to enforce its will; how far, in more sensational language, it menaces or might menace our much-prized liberties. Could the Government, for instance, order the Metropolitan police force to raid the houses of all members of a certain political party? In answering these questions, we must distinguish between the use of the force within and without the Metropolitan police district.

Within the Metropolitan police district, which is inhabited by a fifth of the population of England and Wales, the Government has at its disposal 20,000 men (fewer in practice as the force is seldom up to strength) whom it can use for virtually what purposes it likes, subject only to two instruments of restraint: Parliament and the courts. How effective the restraint of Parliament will be, it is, of course, impossible to say, as this will depend on the amount of support possessed by the Government. A Government with a large and docile majority can do virtually anything, but in other circumstances it will have to be more sensitive to public opinion both within and without Parliament. The restraints imposed by the courts are often said to be effective and substantial, but it is easy to overrate them. It is true that an aggrieved individual may always bring an action against the police officer who has, in his view, exceeded his powers, but even if he wins his case, all that happens is that he is awarded damages. The court cannot restrain members of the force from exceeding their powers on future occasions. If the police officer had exceeded his instructions, or had acted without instructions, he might be put on a disciplinary charge, if the Commissioner so decided, which would at least probably ensure that that particular officer was more careful in future; but this does not, of course, protect the public from police officers acting on instructions from their superiors knowing that they will be supported by them if difficulties ensue. We may therefore conclude that a Government which wanted, for instance, to persecute a certain political party which was organised from or operated in the Metropolitan police district could do so with equanimity on repeated occasions if it felt secure of its majority in Parliament, provided it did not mind running the risk of actions in the courts.

In trying to estimate the value to a Government of this weapon, the Metropolitan police force, it is helpful to compare the position with that in the provinces. A provincial police authority is not, it is true, worried by Parliament, though in so far as it is elected it may be worried by the electors; but, on the other hand, the members of its force have, with a few exceptions, less extensive powers than those possessed by the Metropolitan police particularly in connection with the arrest of persons on suspicion in certain circumstances. There are, perhaps, good grounds for arming the police of the Metropolis with special powers of this kind; in any event the powers are often found useful, and distinguish the force from all provincial forces, except those few which have been given special powers by a local Act of Parliament. Another difference between the Metropolis and the provinces must be mentioned. Whatever the legal position, it would appear that as a matter of practice the Home Secretary would in certain circumstances give directions to the Commissioner regarding the executive acts of the force; i.e. he might order certain premises to be searched or watched. This seldom, if ever, happens in the provinces. Provincial police authorities, as we have seen, do not give orders to their Chief Constables regarding the executive acts of the police, except occasionally during a crisis such as a strike. If a provincial Chief Constable were proposing to search the premises of a political party, he might consult the Home Office before doing so, but it is most unlikely that he would consult his police authority.

But outside the Metropolitan police district, the Home Secretary cannot use his police force unless he is asked to help another force— that is, he cannot in the sense that members of the force do not possess the powers of constables outside the Metropolitan police district and the counties immediately surrounding it, unless they are summoned to help another force under a mutual aid agreement in an emergency, or are being used in connection with the protection of royal palaces. Members of the Special Branch of the Metropolitan force who are stationed at some ports where they work with the Immigration Staff of the Home Office are not sworn in as constables for that locality, and persons detained at the ports are normally detained by the Immigration Officer under the powers he possesses.

There are, therefore, limitations to the use of the Metropolitan police force as a state police, but the situation is nevertheless not without dangers. It is easier for arbitrary acts to go undetected in an enormous town such as London than in a smaller unit, and a person who considers he has been wronged may feel daunted in launching a case against a member of so large an organisation as the Metropolitan police force, supported as it is by legal and other experts. There are other dangers inherent in the size of the force. Bribery and corruption are less easy to detect than in a smaller force, and on the whole are more likely to occur in the Metropolis than elsewhere as the temptations are greater. In an organisation of this size, more 'red tape' is necessary than in a smaller one, and there is a tendency for the machine to become inflexible, official and soulless. Vigilance by the public through Parliament and any other means it can find or devise to keep a careful watch on the activities of the Metropolitan police force is therefore vital if the inhabitants of this country are to retain those liberties of which they are so proud.

CHAPTER VII

Policewomen

T H E employment of women on police duties has, ever since it was first advocated, aroused passions on both sides which seem to the impartial observer out of all proportion to the good or harm they may do. The case for and against policewomen has as a result been grossly overstated. The advocates have appeared to claim that one had only to appoint policewomen for all immorality and juvenile delinquency to vanish. 'There really are no limitations to what one can do', said a woman patrol in evidence before an official committee in 1920. Another witness said, 'A woman's presence always ennobles. She has a very great power within herself that is not force.' Policewomen have been called 'not only a national but a moral necessity'; and an M.P. has claimed that they can arrest drunken men when men cannot. In the multitude of resolutions from women's organisations which have from time to time been sent to the Home Office, equally extravagant claims have been made on behalf of policewomen who nowadays would themselves be the first to admit their limitations.

But their opponents have underestimated their value. In 1920 policewomen were described by an M.P. as an 'extravagant eccentricity' upon whose 'entertainment' public money should not be wasted. During the following 20 years many persons in official positions acted as if they thought likewise, though they were not always so outspoken. Often it was said, at one and the same time, that the duties on which policewomen were employed could be as well if not better carried out by policemen, or by philanthropic ladies not hampered by a police uniform. The magistrate who feels embarrassed by the presence of a policewoman in his court is probably a rare occurrence now; and it would be difficult to find one expressing himself as strongly as Mr. Mead who said in 1920 that policewomen had, in taking up this particular work, 'sterilised any maiden modesty they might have had'; women and children, he added, should not be entrusted to abnormal women of this sort who seemed to suffer from a sort of moral obliquity. But there are still people who, with no doubt the best of motives, wish to protect the interests of women by keeping them from contamination with the degrading subjects with which policewomen often have to deal.

Early History

Women were first employed on police duties in England during the war of 1914–1918. A few had been so employed in some countries (viz. Germany and the U.S.A.) before then; and there had been for many years before 1914 in England 'police matrons' who did such duties as supervising, searching and escorting women and children in custody, but they were not constables, and did no patrol work.

During the early years of the 20th century, many social reformers pressed for the appointment of policewomen, but it was the war that gave women their chance in this as in so many other spheres. There were two main sources of activity for the organisation of women patrols: one was the National Union of Women Workers (which later became the National Council of Women), whose patrols were called the Voluntary Women Patrols; the other was Miss Damer-Dawson, a humanitarian lady who had been specially interested in animal welfare; her patrols, when first started in 1914, were called Women Police Volunteers. The two bodies were always independent of one another, being organised on different lines and having rather different aims, and it is important to distinguish them. Several of the early members of Miss Damer-Dawson's Volunteers had been militant suffragettes, and gave the impression that they were more interested in improving the position of women than in developing some branches of police work. The National Union of Women Workers was also no doubt keen to show what women could do, but they approached the matter more from the point of view of social workers. The Women Police Volunteers zentred round Miss Damer-Dawson until after her death in 1920, when her place was taken by Miss Mary Allen. Miss Allen has claimed that the movement with which she was associated was the begetter of the women's section of the police service, but it would perhaps be nearer the truth to say that women are employed on police duties to-day in spite of, rather than because of, the activities of the Women Police Volunteers.

Soon after the outbreak of war, the National Union of Women Workers, having for a long time been convinced of the need for policewomen, organised voluntary workers who did preventive work amongst women and girls, chiefly by patrolling in the vicinity of military camps and in parks, etc. The Union selected and trained the women, and either sent them out under their auspices or lent them to Chief Constables. Altogether 4,000 to 5,000 women passed through the Union's hands. In some places where their work was particularly appreciated they were paid out of the rates, and gradually they changed from being part-time voluntary workers to whole-time paid ones. In 1916 the Commissioner of Police of the Metropolis took a small number of the Union's patrols into official employment, and women have been employed on police duties in the Metropolitan police district ever since that date.

Miss Damer-Dawson supplied women to many Chief Constables, but her chief work lay in recruiting and training hundreds of women for preventive work in munition factories. Her Women Police Service also did patrol work in London for several years, but not under the control of the Commissioner of Police. Miss Allen has written very indignantly of the refusal of the Commissioner to take on members of the organisation whose training, discipline and experience in her view fitted them for the work. The organisers of the Women Police Service were certainly strict disciplinarians and attached great importance to intensive drilling and to the wearing of uniform. Miss Allen seems usually to have worn riding boots. In some cases their appearance was such that they were mistaken for men, but the truth of the story that one of them was seen wearing a sword seems more doubtful. The Commissioner found that the existence of these unofficial patrols confused the public and led to difficulties, and he prosecuted them under the Police Act, 1919, for wearing uniform resembling that of the police. After that they changed their name again, to Women's Auxiliary Service.

It was unfortunate for the movement for police women that the forces of the protagonists were at first divided; moreover, the association of the Women Police Service with the militant suffragettes tended to discredit in certain circles the whole idea of policewomen. Some of the patrols were said to give the impression they

were there to show policemen how to do their work and to purify
the male police, and it has taken policewomen many years to live
down their reputation as eccentrics and feminists. Nor did their
treatment in the inter-war years as the Cinderella of the police
service encourage them to take a warm-hearted view of many of
their male colleagues.

1920–1929

The Desborough Committee did not concern itself with the
employment of women on police duties, but a special committee—
the Baird Committee—was appointed in 1920 to report on the
matter. This Committee found that the experience of the war had
proved that women could be employed with advantage to the
community in the performance of certain police duties which before
were exclusively discharged by men, and that in thickly populated
areas there was not only scope, but urgent need for the employment of policewomen; but the Committee thought that the
questions whether policewomen should be appointed, and if so how
many, ought to remain at the discretion of the police authority
concerned, and they strongly deprecated any interference with this
discretion. The Home Secretary, when circulating the report to
police authorities, said he thought policewomen could be of great
assistance, but he left their employment entirely to the discretion of
each individual authority. There were at that time 112 policewomen
in the Metropolitan police district, and 126 in the rest of England
and Wales. These were employed by 43 police authorities.

In the light of the terms of the Baird Committee's report and of
the views of the Home Secretary and of the senior Inspector of
Constabulary who was keen to see more women employed, it
seemed probable that numbers would expand and conditions of
service improve. This, however, was not to be. A bad blow was
dealt by the economy campaign of the early 'twenties. In the
light of the Geddes Committee's report, Mr. Shortt, the Home
Secretary, decided in 1922 to disband altogether the women patrols
in London. Many M.P.s were very disturbed at the decision and
pressed strongly for its revocation. They pointed out that the
information before the Geddes Committee was very scanty: only
the Home Secretary and the Commissioner of Police had been consulted; policewomen did not only do welfare work, and it would be

a false economy, and in the long run not even an economy, to disband them. The Home Secretary thought the work policewomen did would continue to be done by voluntary social workers and policemen's wives, but, as Lady Astor pointed out, policemen did not choose their wives with a view to their patrolling the streets or escorting prisoners, and they might often not be qualified, apart from being too busy, to do police work. In the end the Home Secretary relented and agreed to keep a nucleus of 20 women out of the 112 previously engaged. The severe reduction of the women's section of the Metropolitan police force did not encourage other police authorities to appoint or retain women in their forces. Fifteen forces dismissed their women and five reduced the numbers employed. By the autumn of 1922, numbers were down to 87 women employed by 31 provincial authorities.

In 1924 the Home Secretary, Mr. Arthur Henderson, appointed another Committee under the chairmanship of Mr. W. C. Bridgeman to review the employment of women police. There had not in fact been a great deal of experience of policewomen since 1920 when the Baird Committee reported, and the Bridgeman Committee came to very much the same conclusions, namely, that the efficiency of the police service had been improved by the employment of women, but that each police authority should have an absolute discretion as to whether or not to employ any. The 1924 committee was, however, rather less enthusiastic about the value of policewomen than the 1920 committee and this had some effect on the future. The Bridgeman report was brought to the attention of police authorities, but the implementation of its recommendations, both as regards employing any women at all and as regards their conditions of service, was left entirely to the discretion of police authorities.

Whether as a result of the recommendation of the Bridgeman Committee or not, the establishment of policewomen in the Metropolitan police force was in 1924 raised from 22 to 50. Apart from this there is little to record for the years 1924–1929. The Home Secretary, Sir. W. Joynson-Hicks, was frequently pressed from many quarters to give police authorities a lead and to encourage or even instruct them to employ policewomen, especially in large industrial towns, but he always said the matter must be left to the discretion of police authorities. He even went so far on one occasion as to say that legislation would be necessary before he could bring pressure to bear on police authorities on such an issue, and that in any case he disliked the exercise of any powers he had over 'these great local authorities' which he thought would be 'an infringement of the right of local self-government'. Mr. Clynes, as Home Secretary from 1929–1931, was anxious to encourage the employment of policewomen, where there was scope for them, but apart from increasing the numbers employed in London, he did not succeed in doing much.

Attestation as Constables

One of the first questions which arose in connection with the employment of women on police duties was whether they could be attested as constables. The issue is an interesting one as it throws light on what is entailed by the office of constable. During the years 1914–1918 the Home Office advised that as women were physically incapable of discharging the duties incumbent by law on a constable, they ought not to be allowed to pledge themselves to do so. A number of women were, nevertheless, attested as constables even before the Sex Disqualification (Removal) Act, 1919, dispelled any legal doubts on the matter. After 1919 the argument turned on the issue whether it was necessary and desirable to attest them. All the policewomen who appeard before the Baird Committee and a large number of other witnesses strongly urged that they should be given the status and powers of constable to enable them to extend their work and give them a greater sense of security. On the other hand, it was said that it was hardly ever necessary or desirable for a policewoman (or indeed for a policeman) to exercise any greater powers of arrest than those conferred by common law on all citizens. In that case, the women asked, why were the men attested? The Baird Committee recommended a compromise: that policewomen should make the declaration of a constable in the same form as the men, but that the duties they would and would not be primarily expected to perform should be prescribed by regulations made by the police authority.

Metropolitan policewomen were attested as constables from 1923 onwards, but many forces were slow to act on the Baird Committee's recommendation, no doubt partly because the Home Office did not encourage them to do so. The question was reopened in 1924 by the Bridgeman Committee. The old arguments were gone

over again and the committee simply recommended that policewomen should make the declaration of a constable.

Even then in many areas policewomen were not attested for some
time: one-third of the policewomen employed by provincial police
authorities in 1930 were not attested, and in 1939 the proportion
was still as high as one-sixth. Some police authorities were suspected
of being against the attestation of women because they hoped thus
to avoid paying them pensions. During the second world war
things went to the other extreme, and in some areas auxiliary policewomen were, wrongly it would seem, attested as constables even
though they were mainly employed on indoor duties and were not
qualified to perform the duties of constables. To-day there are no
auxiliary policewomen left, and all the regular policewomen are
attested.

1929–1939

The general question of policewomen and in particular the preventive side of their work were not within the terms of reference of
the Royal Commission on Police Powers and Procedure (1929),
but they considered the employment of women police in the
investigation of crimes and offences, and they in fact made a fairly
thorough enquiry into the matter. They pointed out that the
experience gained with regard to the ways in which policewomen
could suitably be employed was far more extensive and valuable
than the small number of policewomen then serving (150 in England
and none in Wales) would seem to indicate. The Commission was
satisfied that the time was ripe for a substantial increase in the
numbers of policewomen, more particularly in cities for patrol work
in uniform, and to take statements from all young girls and children
in sexual cases. It also recommended that policewomen should be
afforded adequate opportunities of doing general, as well as special
detective work, and suggested that women might usefully be
employed on many of the miscellaneous and extraneous duties
which had to be performed by the police. The Commission was in
general agreement with the policy hitherto adopted by the Home
Secretary of leaving to local discretion the decision whether or not to
employ policewomen, and in what ways; but it added that if the
views it expressed commended themselves to the public, it hoped
the Home Secretary would call the attention of all Chief Constables

and police authorities to the marked success with which policewomen had been employed in various parts of the country and to
the good results which would follow from an increase in their
numbers. It appears from the Royal Commission's report that unofficial
organisations of 'policewomen' still existed at that date. The Commission expressed the view that, while these organisations deserved
much credit for pioneer work, they were not readily understood or
accepted by the public at large, and that if the number of official
policewomen was increased, the need for the unofficial organisations would diminish. Similar views had been expressed, but rather
more emphatically, nine years before by the Baird Committee.

There was, however, very little change in the numbers and
duties of policewomen during the next 10 years, except in the
Metropolitan police force, and even there development was very
slow. The Home Secretary gave authority in 1929 to recruit up to
100 women for the Metropolitan police force, but before the increase
had been made, the economy campaign of the early 'thirties had
started, and the abolition of 'this new and dainty luxury' as an
M.P. described policewomen was again recommended. It was not
until 1938 that London had 100 policewomen, a number it had not
had since 1921. In the provinces, from 1929 to 1939 the number of
policewomen rose very little, from 99 to 119, and only four more
police authorities employed women in 1939 than in 1929; 137 out of
the 181 forces did not employ any.

It may be asked why so little progress was made in the inter-war
years. Three Committees had reported in favour of the employment
of policewomen, two of them quite enthusiastically; Sir Leonard
Dunning, who was an Inspector of Constabulary from 1912 to
1930, thought they did useful work, some of which could not be
done by policemen; most Chief Constables who had experience of
them were in their favour; and their extended use was constantly
recommended by most, if not all, of the women's organisations in
the country who were concerned with criminal or social work. But
the explanation is not difficult. Many police authorities were
deterred by the cost; others considered that there was nothing a
policeman could not do better or, at any rate, as well as a policewoman, and that the work policewomen did was welfare work
which should be done by voluntary bodies. These views were

K 2

shared by many Chief Constables, who had little experience of women at work, even as clerks or typists. For in many forces most if not all of the clerical and typing work was done by men, often policemen, until the war of 1939–1945; indeed some Chief Constables were astonished when they found during the second world war that women could type quite efficiently. Nor were they brought into contact with women in responsible posts in the Home Office until the war. Moreover, the case for policewomen was overstated by their protagonists, and it was often suspected that they were motivated by feminism rather than by a desire to see police work done in the best possible way. Nor did many of the organisations which pressed for the appointment of policewomen appear to recognise the limitations of police powers or the undesirability of the police concerning themselves with private morals. The result was that the question was discussed with prejudice on both sides and seldom on its merits.

But the single most important factor was probably the attitude of the Home Office. All Home Secretaries between the wars maintained that the need for employing women must be determined by the local police authority in the light of local conditions and that the Home Secretary was not in a position to bring any pressure on police authorities in this matter. They could point to the recommendations to this effect made by various committees, but it would seem that the Home Secretary could have given a lead if he had felt disposed to do so, without exceeding the proper bounds of his authority. To those who came on deputations it appeared as if the permanent officials thought there was little scope for policewomen and did not wish to see more of them employed. Certainly if this was the view of the Home Office, its passive policy was ideal for the purpose and had the added advantage that it could be defended on sound constitutional principles. And even those officials such as Sir L. Dunning who wished to see their use extended, thought that the matter should be left to the discretion of the local police authorities, not on grounds of expediency for fear of antagonising the authorities, but because they 'must be the best judges' of the need for policewomen. 'No central authority for instance can say whether the police authority which prefers to grant a subsidy to an outside organisation to appointing policewomen is right or wrong.' (H.M. Inspector's Report, 1925.) A very different attitude to the legitimate rôle of the central authority was to be taken 20 years later.

Pay and Conditions of Service

Nor did the Home Office take the lead in improving the pay and conditions of service of the women who were employed. Until 1931 the women were in the same position as the men before 1919, in that pay and conditions of service varied from force to force and were often very poor. The National Council of Women and various other organisations urged from 1919 onwards that the pay and conditions of service of policewomen should be standardised by the Home Secretary and that policewomen should be represented on the Police Council. The Baird Committee also recommended the standardisation of pay, at lower rates than the men's, and that conditions of service should with a few exceptions be identical to the men's. The Home Secretary did not make regulations embodying these recommendations. It is not surprising, therefore, that the Bridgeman Committee found in 1924 that in 20 out of the 34 forces employing policewomen, they received less pay than was recommended by the Baird Committee (60s. to 80s. a week); in one force it was as low as 35s. to 45s. a week. The Bridgeman Committee recommended that in order to attract the right class of woman to the police service the rates of pay recommended in 1920 should be generally adopted and that women should receive the same allowances as men.

But the Home Secretary did not regulate policewomen's conditions of service until 1931. In that year he prescribed standard scales of pay and conditions of service, and the duties on which women might particularly be employed. He also applied the men's discipline code to the women and laid down the conditions on which they might be promoted. At the same time a policewoman was allowed to attend the Police Council. These developments were regarded by policewomen as a great move forward. Conditions of service improved in some respects: for instance, women became entitled, like their male colleagues, to rent allowances which they had not always received before then. One of the main obstacles to progress had been the fact that with poor and uncertain conditions of service, it was difficult to recruit suitable women for the work, and the appointment of unsuitable ones, of course, discredited the species. Promotion prospects improved slightly with the creation in 1931 and 1932 of the first four posts of Woman Inspector in the provincial forces. There were in 1939 still only four such posts in provincial forces, and six in the Metropolitan police force. Apart from one Superintendent, there were no higher posts for women. There was thus no outlet at the top to Assistant Chief Constable, Chief Constable and H.M. Inspector as in the case of the men, and promotion was as a result extremely slow. The prospects for a keen woman were very poor. They have improved considerably during the last few years.

Nor did policewomen have the assistance of the Police Federation in altering their conditions. Legally every attested policewoman, being a member of a police force, is *ipso facto* a member of the Federation, but in fact, until just recently, the Federation has refused to represent the interests of policewomen. In a few forces women were allowed by their male colleagues to take part in the election of the Branch Boards, but the central organisation of the Federation refused to take action on any representations regarding policewomen which were made by a Branch Board. There has never been a woman member of one of the Central Committees. Nor did the women have any separate facilities for collective representation. Scattered about all over the country in very small numbers, they seldom if ever met each other, and had almost no opportunities for discussing their common problems; the few who protested individually were unable to make any impression on the Federation and were frowned upon by their senior officers. Even H.M. Inspectors appeared to take little interest in their work or conditions. On one occasion in 1937 an enterprising woman got permission to organise a meeting of all policewomen in the country, but they were forbidden by the Home Office to discuss their conditions of service. At no time, however, until recently did the Home Office bring any pressure to bear on the Federation to allow women to exercise their rights of membership.

In their evidence before the committee of 1920, the Federation spoke in favour of the employment of women on police duties, but by 1922 they were already passing resolutions against women and ever since then until recently they have been opposed to their employment. Amongst the many grounds for their opposition, there were the usual ones that the work could be better done by policemen or by voluntary organisations in touch with the police, and that to employ women in police offices deprived policemen of useful experience. They also feared that their employment would prejudice the chances of disabled men. Rather less explicit was the argument advanced by a representative of the Federation before the Bridgeman Committee that 'the very nature of the duties of a police constable are contrary to that which is finest and best in woman'.

1939-1949

These 20 years of disheartening, uphill struggle were to be succeeded by sensational, almost too rapid, changes. Once again a war provided the impetus which, it seemed, nothing else would. First of all in 1939 the Women's Auxiliary Police Corps was formed. Most of its members were not employed on police duties proper, e.g. patrolling or detective work, but on auxiliary work, e.g. clerical, typing, canteen and driving duties. A few of them were gradually given more responsible work, and by the middle of the war were performing the duties of regular policewomen. The use of women in far larger numbers than previously for all these duties did much to break down the ignorance and prejudice which obtained in many quarters of the police service regarding the capacities of women. At its peak in 1943 the Corps numbered 4,500 whole-time members. Although it has now been disbanded, women are employed in many more police offices on work for which they are specially suited than before the war, and the Corps accustomed Chief Constables and others to working with them.

Secondly, war conditions involving a general upheaval of social conditions led to insistent demands in many quarters for the appointment of more policewomen for patrol duties. In August, 1940, police authorities were asked by the Home Secretary to consider afresh whether in the light of war conditions there was a need in their districts for more policewomen or auxiliaries, especially in districts where there were large military establishments or munition factories. No pressure, however, was put on police authorities at this time, and during the next four years the number of regular policewomen increased by only 80. The increase would undoubtedly have been greater if it had been easier to recruit suitable women. By the spring of 1944 public opinion had been aroused, and for the first time the Home Secretary insisted that all forces in areas where large numbers of troops were concentrated should include some policewomen who would help to maintain standards of order and decorum. If the police authorities in the areas concerned did not appoint some women, they might find themselves directed to do so under the Defence Regulations. A large number of authorities decided to employ women or more women, both regulars and auxiliaries, in response to this circular, and although many could not recruit up to the figures aimed at, numbers increased substantially. Policewomen became the craze. The most astonishing conversions occurred amongst police authorities and Chief Constables, whether from conviction or expediency was not always clear.

Further stimulus was provided by the appointment in 1945 of a female staff officer to the Inspectors of Constabulary to inspect policewomen and make recommendations with regard to their efficiency and to advise Chief Constables on the matter. This had been recommended by the Baird and Bridgeman Committees and for many years by women's organisations. A few Chief Constables did not at first take kindly to having some of their force inspected by a woman, but prejudices were rapidly dispelled and the appointment was soon recognised as of great benefit to the police service. Most Chief Constables were pleased to get advice on the selection of recruits and on the best use to make of their policewomen, and the women themselves at last felt that someone was taking an interest in their work and conditions of service and that they had a spokesman in the Home Office.

It is, nevertheless, remarkable to find a committee of 30 persons, all of whom were Chief Officers of police, H.M. Inspectors, or officials of the Home Office and Scottish Office, recommending in 1946 that every police force should henceforth employ some police-women, unless the police authority or Chief Constable, after consultation with the Inspector, could satisfy the Secretary of State that the circumstances were so exceptional as to make the principle inapplicable in that particular district. But this is what the Police Post-War Committee recommended. Perhaps more remarkable is the fact that this recommendation has been implemented. A steady rise has taken place during the last few years in the numbers of policewomen authorised and employed, and in the number of police authorities employing them, as the following figures will show.

Year	Policewomen					Police authorities	
	EMPLOYED			Total employed	Total authorised	Employing policewomen	Not employing police-women
	Counties	Boroughs	Met. police force				
1939	32	87	127	246	—	45	138
1945	104	169	133	406	—	67	92
1946	236	254	131	621	1,133	100	59
1947	340	309	181	830	1,249	111	20
1948	405	380	211	996	1,360	123	7
1949	449	439	260*	1,148	1,553	130	—

* Including four in the City of London.

It will be seen that the numbers employed in the Metropolitan police district have not risen as steeply as the numbers in the provinces. In 1939 over half all policewomen were employed in London; in 1949 the proportion was less than a quarter. One would expect to find more policewomen in a large town such as London, but it appears to be more difficult to recruit women for the Metropolitan police force than for most other forces.

The Federation, too, has moved with the times, though not without some prodding by the Home Secretary. In 1947 the central bodies of the Federation agreed that their constitution as laid down in the Police Act, 1919, should be 'interpreted as including all police officers of the federated ranks irrespective of sex'; since then policewomen have taken part in the Federation's work and representations have been made on their behalf, but its constitution should be altered to ensure that women are represented by their own sex at the various levels of the machinery.

Another important development has been the great improvement which has been effected in the training of policewomen. Before the war one or two forces, including the Metropolitan force, maintained training schools for their women recruits and accepted at these schools recruits from other forces. But it was left entirely to the discretion of each police authority and Chief Constable whether to send their policewomen to schools, and many of them did not. Some policewomen had been trained by one of the voluntary organisations which functioned during the war of 1914–1918, but even they could have done with a more up-to-date training. A few policewomen were trained with male recruits, but several were simply left to pick up what they could from their colleagues. Some policewomen performed wonders considering their lack of training, but it seems clear that they would have benefited by a better grounding in police duties, and have been a better advertisement of the cause. Since 1945 all women recruits have been trained with male recruits at the Home Office District Training Schools. Apart from a few specialised classes in their particular duties, the women receive the same training as the men, an arrangement which acclimatises the male recruit to the idea of a female colleague and starts them off on a footing of equality.

At one time many police authorities did not preclude married women from appointment to the force, and the Baird and Bridgeman Committees did not recommend their exclusion. The Home Secretary's regulations of 1931, however, required policewomen to be unmarried or widows. This provision was repealed in 1946. It is not astonishing to find married women excluded from the police at a time when they were not accepted in the Civil Service, or, in many areas, as teachers. The strange thing is that the marriage bar was abolished in the police service before it was abolished in the Civil Service even though there are greater practical difficulties in having married women in the police than in the Civil Service. This may have been done as much to assist with recruiting and to eliminate wastage amongst trained policewomen, as on the ground that a married woman should in certain respects be more suited to a policewoman's duties than an unmarried one. There are, no doubt, still some police officers who consider that married policewomen should not be permitted on the ground that it is bad for a man not to have to maintain his wife, or that a woman's place is in the home, but they have for the time being at any rate lost their battle.

Equal Pay

'Equal pay' to policewomen has not yet been granted. The rates for female constables and sergeants are 9·5 per cent. to 12 per cent. lower than the men's rates; in the case of inspectors, the difference is greater: 15 per cent. Policewomen receive allowances, however, at broadly the same rates as policemen. The Royal Commission on Equal Pay (1946) pointed out that policewomen have exactly the same powers as men and that any constable must in fact deal with any situation demanding action by the police which may confront him or her. The Commission considered that policemen and women 'are employed on essentially the same work', subject to the fact that men only are used for certain duties, such as controlling traffic, quelling riots and controlling crowds, and that there are certain duties for which women are considered specially suitable, e.g. duties in connection with women and children; but that while over a wide range of duties men and women are 'similarly employed', it is seldom possible to replace the individual male constable by a policewoman.

The Royal Commission made no specific recommendation regarding the police, and this is not the place to make more than one or two remarks on a question which raises many complex issues of general importance. But this much can be said. The case for equal pay for men and women in the police service is not as strong as in various other occupations, e.g. the Civil Service, where for most of the work men and women are recruited on a common examination regardless of their sex. In these occupations they may truly be said to be interchangeable. In the police, on the other hand, a Chief Constable or police authority sets out to recruit so many men and so many women, and normally if the establishment of policewomen in a particular force is increased, no corresponding reduction is made in the establishment of men. This incidentally may at a time of acute manpower shortage account for some of the popularity of policewomen amongst Chief Constables. It is also broadly speaking true that whereas policemen can do policewomen's work (except some things, such as searching female prisoners), though in some cases perhaps not so effectively, there are certain sides of policemen's work which policewomen cannot do because of their lesser physical capacity. These may perhaps not be so numerous as some people think, but, nevertheless, it is obvious that unless changes take place in the physical characteristics of the two sexes as they exist in Western Europe to-day, there will always be duties which policemen are more fitted to undertake than policewomen. On the other hand, for certain types of police duty—clerical work or some detective and enquiry work—policemen and women are interchangeable and they can properly be said to be doing 'equal work'. The case for equal pay is then stronger, but it would lead to difficulties if policewomen employed on such duties were paid at a higher rate than those employed on other duties, e.g. patrol work.

It is sometimes suggested that policewomen should receive the same pay as policemen because they do work of 'equal value'. But little can be founded on this argument. Things do not have a value apart from that which people attach to them. The economic value of policewomen's services is the wage for which they will work. This wage is not left for determination by the forces of supply and demand, but is fixed by the Home Secretary, perhaps with, perhaps without, regard to supply and demand. If less pay were offered, fewer suitable women might be forthcoming for the work; or they might not. If more pay were offered, more, and more suitable, women might be forthcoming; or they might not. But there seems no reason to think that in the circumstances of to-day it is more difficult to recruit for the pay offered the numbers and types of policewomen than the numbers and types of policemen required. There are, however, different criteria for estimating value. Some people attach considerable moral or social value to policewomen's services and consider that people doing work of great moral or social value should be highly paid. One cannot say that this view is right or wrong; it is as legitimate as any other. Or it might be argued that what should be rewarded is running risks of physical (not moral) danger, an argument which points to higher rates for policemen than for policewomen, at any rate in peace-time. We may take what criteria we like for estimating the value of services, but there seems no good reason for saying that because a policewoman does not perform the *same* work as a policeman she is worth less : we might regard her as worth more. To the fact that few demands for equal pay from policewomen have been heard, little can be attributed, as they have until recently had no representative organisation for putting forward their views, and they are now represented almost wholly by men.

Conclusion

In 10 years' time it will be easier than it is now to make a proper assessment of the usefulness of policewomen and of the numbers which it is desirable to employ in the different types of area. This cannot be done yet as it is only recently that they have been appointed in considerable numbers and have been properly trained and given a chance to show what they can do. One can, however, form certain conclusions about the duties for which they are suitable. At one time a great deal of emphasis was laid on the value of policewomen in cases of sexual offences involving women and children, and in some areas they have been mainly used on such work. It now seems apparent that they are capable of doing many other types of work as well, and it is obviously undesirable in the interests of the policewomen that they should be mainly or exclusively employed in dealing with the more sordid type of police work. Moreover, in some instances a woman victim is more likely to give the necessary information to a policeman than to a policewoman. In most forces there are not enough policewomen to employ them on all cases in which women and children are concerned as victims or offenders, but it is possible to employ them on many of these. They are particularly suitable for investigating 'care and protection' and child neglect cases. Women have also shown considerable aptitude for general detective work. A woman may look at a problem from a different angle to a man or may have some useful knowledge of the habits of women which a man has not. Patrol work in special districts, e.g. where young persons hang about and girls get into trouble, policewomen are particularly suited to perform, but they should patrol in all types of district from time to time to get a good all-round knowledge of their police area. There are other obvious duties for which women must be used, e.g. searching and escorting female prisoners, and any policewoman worth her pay will find that she is often asked for advice by, for example, women and girls in difficulties, or mothers who cannot control their children. But it is clear that even when full weight has been given to the duties which may well be performed by women, the police service must remain preponderantly a masculine service. Over the country as a whole in 1949 women constitute nearly 2 per cent. of the total police strength. Some people consider saturation point has been reached. Others would like to see the percentage rise during the next decade or so to about 5 per cent., at any rate in urban areas. One of the factors which will determine whether or not this will happen will no doubt be the general economic condition of the country. For if times are bad there is pressure to give the jobs to the men, and a tendency to regard policewomen as a luxury. Perhaps one day they will be taken on instead of men because they are cheaper.

Much of the work performed by policewomen borders on moral welfare work, and it is important to try to decide where police work should end and moral welfare work begin. Many acts of immorality do not lead to a breach of the peace or the commission of an offence against the law, and it is generally speaking important that the police, whether men or women, should not concern themselves with these matters. Many of the organisations which press for the appointment of policewomen often do not appear to recognise the limitations of police powers or the undesirability of the police concerning themselves with private morals.

On the other hand, behaviour which may appear not to be strictly speaking the concern of the police may lead to a breach of the peace or the commission of an offence; for example, immorality may involve indecency constituting a criminal offence and thus requiring action by the police. Moreover, behaviour which in relation to adults does not constitute an offence against the criminal law may well do so in the case of young persons. And last but not least, the police have a duty to prevent as well as to detect crime. In the opening words of the Metropolitan Police Instruction Book, 'The primary object of an efficient police is the prevention of crime; the next that of detection and punishment of offenders, if crime is committed.' But when policewomen do preventive work, many people call it 'rescue work' and say that it should be done by other bodies. There is the further consideration that much of this border-line preventive work, if not done by the police, is not done at all. For most voluntary moral welfare organisations have slender financial resources. Their work could often be more effectively performed by members of a police force who have had the benefit of police training and whose uniform carries authority and is a safeguard in the eyes of the public against unwarranted interference.

How far these conflicting considerations can be resolved is a difficult question of policy which must take into account the state of public opinion at the time, which is not necessarily identical with the views expressed by the more vocal protagonists of either of the two extreme schools of thought. Thus it was right during the war that policewomen should take a broad view of their functions and undertake work which bordered on moral welfare work. In normal times, on the other hand, the best interests of the police and public will be served if policewomen are made an integral part of the police service and are employed on the traditional duties of the police, leaving moral welfare to other agencies, except, of course, in the case of young persons with whose welfare the law is concerned.

CHAPTER VIII

Recruitment, Training
and Promotion

The Discretion to Recruit

NOTHING illustrates the autonomy of British police forces better than the fact that each Chief Officer or police authority is absolutely free to choose the members of their force, provided certain qualifying conditions laid down in the Home Secretary's regulations are satisfied. The regulations provide that nobody may be appointed a member of a police force unless he or she is: (1) within certain age limits; (2) not less than a stated height; (3) of good character and with a satisfactory record in past employments; (4) physically and mentally fitted to perform the duties of a constable; and (5) sufficiently well educated. It will be seen that the last three out of these five conditions are matters of opinion, not matters of fact. A man who appears to one Chief Constable fit to be a police officer might not so appear to another Chief Constable or to the Home Secretary; but the appointing authority, whether Chief Constable or police authority, has complete discretion on these matters: the Home Secretary cannot prevent the appointment of any man or woman as a police officer if the age and height qualifications are satisfied, and these, incidentally, he can waive. There is, of course, a wide measure of agreement as to what qualities fit or do not fit a man for the police: for instance, honesty, tact and clear-headedness are generally thought to be desirable characteristics; but, nevertheless, there are certain matters about which opinions differ. Thus some Chief Constables prefer brawn to brain and distrust a man who has had a good education; others show a strong preference for ex-service men. The ideal force is probably composed of men of all types: the educated man is useful for office work; the intelligent man of the world should make a good detective; the athlete and tough ex-sergeant major will be useful in control of other men or where physical courage or force is required.

The power to appoint members of a borough force is, as we have seen, vested by law in the Watch Committee, but normally the Chief Constable selects recruits, and confirmation by the committee is a purely formal process. In all other forces, the power to appoint is vested in the Chief Officer, and he will select the members of his force subject in larger forces to a certain amount of delegation of this authority to subordinates.

The discretion of the Chief Officer or police authority to select whom they like for their force is almost as complete now as it has always been. Certain qualifying conditions have been laid down by the Home Secretary for the counties since 1839, and for the boroughs since 1920, but they do not even now limit at all severely the discretion of the appointing authority. This discretion is a very important ingredient of the British system of independent forces. It is true that the forces could remain independent in a system under which men were recruited by some central authority and allocated to the various forces; once allocated they would be members of the local force, not of a national police force, and would be subject, as now, only to the directions of the Chief Officer or police authority for that force as regards their duties. This was the position of the men who were recruited for the police under the National Service Act during the war of 1939–1945; but if such a measure were made permanent, it would destroy one of the most prized rights of Chief Officers and police authorities.

A system under which each force takes independent steps to secure recruits when vacancies occur has, however, certain disadvantages. It leads to undesirable competition and duplication, and to the loss of some applicants who are discouraged when their applications to the forces to which they first apply are for some reason unsuccessful. Moreover, the absence of any co-ordinating machinery may well result in the appointment to some forces of candidates less suitable than those who have failed to be appointed elsewhere. It was obvious that the disadvantages of this system would have been intensified during the years immediately following the end of the war (in 1945) when the intake into the forces was to be far greater than usual to make up deficiencies. Eight District recruiting boards were therefore set up under Home Office guidance to put applicants in touch with forces and to see that no applicant who complied with the general requirements was finally rejected until he had been considered by several forces. This simple and rather obvious piece of machinery was at first viewed with suspicion by some Chief Constables and police authorities who thought, wrongly, that their discretion to appoint whom they liked to their force was being tampered with, but as time went on the boards were generally thought to perform a desirable service. Moreover, it would seem that there is need even in normal times for some machinery of this kind to deal with the applicant who has no preference for any particular force, and to direct to a force where there are vacancies the applicant who, though generally suitable, cannot for some reason be accepted by the force to which he first applies.

The Rate of Recruitment

Before the war of 1939–1945, the average annual intake of the police forces of England and Wales was about 3,000. The average intake aimed at for each of the three years from 1946 to 1948 was nearly four times as great, namely, over 11,000. Most of these recruits were required in order to make up the deficiencies due to the war when recruitment of regular policemen ceased, and to fill the places of the many who retired at the end of the war. But some of the recruits (6,000 out of the total of 34,000 aimed at during the years 1946–1948) were required to expand the pre-war strength of the service. This was thought to be necessary to enable the police to cope with the greater responsibilities which were placed on them after the war. Moreover, when it is said that it is more difficult to recruit policemen now than in the past, it must be remembered that we have been aiming to have not only a greater absolute number of police (22 per cent. more in 1948 than in 1921), but a greater percentage of the population as policemen, as the following figures will show.

Year	Authorised establishment	Population of England and Wales	Population per authorised police officer	Authorised police as percentage of population
1921	56,910	37,885,240	666	·150
1937	61,060	39,950,640	654	·153
1939	63,230	39,950,640	632	·158
1948	69,430	42,750,000	617	·162

The increase in the last column may be regarded as too small to be significant, but it must be remembered that it is difficult to find that combination of physical, mental and moral characteristics which are required in the policeman and that the search for 16 instead of 15 policemen in every 10,000 of the population may make the task appreciably more difficult. During the years between the wars, there were always over 1,000 vacancies in the police, and whilst one cannot assume that all of these were not filled because suitable applicants were not forthcoming, this was probably so in a large number of cases. Applicants, on the other hand, were not lacking. The average number of applications received by the Metropolitan police alone annually for some years before 1939 was 29,000, of whom about 1,000 were normally accepted.

Twenty-four thousand men were in all actually recruited during the years 1946–1948. This was about two and a half times the pre-war rate, and even forces in which a serious deficiency remains like the Metropolitan have been recruiting faster than was usual before the war. It seems improbable that the forces and the training schools could have dealt with a larger number of recruits. Indeed the intake of each force was for various reasons limited by the Home Secretary for two years after the war. It is not the failure to recruit, but the loss by resignations and retirement that is the chief cause of the shortage of policemen in 1949.

The Training of Recruits

Training to-day is the rage—not only for the police, but for all occupations. During and since the last war we have witnessed a torrent of training schemes and undoubtedly many unimaginable feats have been performed. The most unpromising material has been transformed into tools of some use. But there is a danger lest in our craze for training we overlook the importance of common sense, judgment and experience, lest training is thought of as a mechanical process which can turn anyone into anything, if the course is intensive enough. Rather we should think of it as a top dressing which should only be applied with discrimination to a foundation laid by a broad general education.

But in the police service this fashion in training is in the main a healthy reaction against the lack of training given to recruits and to police officers at any stage in their career for many years. Until 1945 the responsibility for training recruits rested on each Chief Constable. In the larger forces, it had been the habit for many years to provide training courses most of which were reasonably good, but it was naturally impossible for the smaller forces to run courses for perhaps one or two recruits at a time. It was also more difficult in rural than in urban areas. Apart from these difficulties which were intrinsic to the system, much more attention was given to training in some forces than in others. Some Chief Constables thought it was sufficient for new recruits, after perhaps a few words from a senior officer, simply to go out on the beat with another constable and pick up what they could as they went along. In the words of H.M. Inspector in 1919, training was and always had been 'utterly inadequate' in many forces. Several witnesses before the Desborough Committee recommended the establishment of central training depôts—very much on the lines of those we have to-day —but others favoured leaving the responsibility with each Chief Constable, in some cases because they feared training schools would enable police officers to compare their conditions of service and thus foster discontent. The committee recommended that the responsibility should be left with Chief Constables, but that the Home Secretary should secure certain standards and a considerable degree of uniformity by regulation.

The Home Secretary made no regulations about training, but between the wars H.M. Inspectors did what they could to improve the standard of training and to impress on Chief Constables that all recruits should be formally trained and not just allowed to pick things up under guidance. Considerable improvements were effectedi n many areas, but by 1939 there were still a few forces which did not send their recruits to any training school. About 40 out of the 183 forces which existed in 1939 maintained training schools of their own. The largest was the Metropolitan training school where there were normally about 200 recruits under instruction. Other schools for 75 to 150 recruits were maintained by about six of the largest forces, but most of the schools were quite small, with a single class of about 20 students. Some operated for part of the year only. Very few were residential. The method, content and quality of the training varied widely.

Here, again, the circumstances of the post-war period provided the immediate stimulant to change. It was obvious that the existing schools could not cope with two or three times the number of recruits they had handled in the past. Arrangements were therefore made to set up nine temporary training centres to which all recruits were to be sent. The schools run by separate forces which had closed during the war were not to take any more recruits, but were to give refresher courses for policemen returning from the armed forces and others. A Central Advisory Committee on which police authorities and Chief Constables were represented was made responsible for the general character of recruit training, and each training school was put under the detailed control of selected Chief Constables from the district. Representatives of police authorities now sit on these management committees as well as Chief Constables. The staff of the schools are appointed by the Home Office on the advice of the local management committees and the premises are owned and equipped by the Home Office; the financial arrangements for splitting the cost between central and local funds were described in chapter IV. It is difficult to make any close comparison between the pre-war and post-war costs of training as full particulars of the pre-war costs are not available, but it would seem probable that the present system is more expensive, even allowing for the fall in the value of money. This is probably due to a higher level of instruction than the average in the training schools before the war, and to the fact that the courses cover more subjects. Police authorities not unnaturally complain of the cost and some of the larger authorities who ran their own schools would like to go back to the pre-war system. It is, of course, unfortunate that so much should be spent on training those many recruits who do not stay long in the police; but on the whole the schools have been adjudged very satisfactory. They were instituted temporarily at first, but in 1948 the Police Authority Associations asked that they should be established on a permanent basis provided police authorities were given a greater share in the management and financial control of the schools, both centrally and locally. Steps have been taken to this end.

The new system of compulsory training is one of the most important changes in police administration which have been made for many years. Successful though the schools have been, however, it may be worth asking whether there is any connection between the high rate of wastage among the police since 1946 and the training given at the schools, for it seems possible that the training is so interesting that it encourages recruits to have too high an expectation of what they will have to do in the police. The courses, which are all residential, last three months. They aim at giving police recruits (men and women) a general picture of the police service and the courts, and a ground-work in the law with which they will be mainly concerned. The danger is lest the courses cover too much ground with resulting indigestion. It is very difficult for some of the recruits to absorb all, or even a reasonable amount, of what they are taught, and it is important that they should not be crammed with information and made to feel they can never learn all they have to know. It is reassuring to know that the Home Office and Inspectors of Constabulary are thinking about these matters, continually revising the courses for instructors and experimenting generally in educational methods.

A recruit on leaving the school goes back to the force to which he belongs and comes under the control of his Chief Constable. He will probably start work at once, though he will be under supervision for a time and will be regarded as receiving training specially in practical work for the next year or so. He remains on probation for two years from his appointment and during that time his services may be dispensed with if the Chief Officer considers that he is not fit physically or mentally to be a policeman. The recruit is normally sent back to the school during the first two years of his service for a short period of further training.

Promotion

With very few exceptions, which will be discussed later, all appointments to the police are made to the lowest rank, that of constable. This is not required by regulation, but it has been the practice for many years. Promotion above the rank of constable is, however, circumscribed by the Home Secretary's regulations. These prescribe that a constable may not be promoted to sergeant unless he has served for five years as a constable and has passed certain examinations. Similarly a sergeant may not be promoted to inspector until he has served for two years as a sergeant and has passed certain further examinations. These conditions may be modified in certain very exceptional circumstances. Promotion to the ranks above inspector is not subject to any statutory conditions.

The examinations which members of the two lower ranks have to pass before they can be considered for promotion are in educational subjects and in police duties. These examinations are in England and Wales set by the several forces independently and there is a wide and unfortunate diversity in the standards required. In Scotland, on the other hand, candidates from all forces take a common examination set and marked by a central board.

These promotion examinations are only qualifying examinations: passing the examination gives no right to promotion, but admits a man into the field of selection. It is generally considered, no doubt rightly, that the qualities necessary in a sergeant or inspector—such as zeal, resourcefulness, leadership and the power to maintain discipline—cannot be tested by orthodox written examinations, but must be gauged by superior officers with knowledge of the officer's conduct and general ability as shown in the performance of police duty over a period. Except in the Metropolitan police, promotion is therefore by selection, subject to the qualifying conditions. It is impossible to say to what extent promotion is by seniority and to what extent by merit where the two do not coincide. Practice varies from force to force, often according to the age of the Chief Officer. He is, as we have seen, the promoting authority in all county forces and in the Metropolitan and City of London forces, and in a borough the Watch Committee is usually guided by the advice of the Chief Constable.

Promotion in the Metropolitan police force has always presented special difficulties because the force is so large that no one officer or group of officers can get to know all the men concerned well enough to decide who amongst the eligible should be promoted. To avoid too much stress being placed on seniority, a system of promotion zones was in force for many years after the first world war. Under this scheme, promotions were limited to men within a zone of selection. If at the end of a certain period a man within the zone had not been promoted, he dropped out of the zone and could not thereafter be promoted. The scheme was intended to reduce and limit the average age of constables and sergeants on promotion, but in fact it worked in the contrary direction, though at the same time it removed from many officers all incentive to promotion. The scheme was abolished in 1947. Another change was also made then. It was decided to make the majority of promotions by competitive (not qualifying) examinations. The reason for this is obvious: it is to give every officer an equal chance of advancement and to remove any suspicion that promotion is by favouritism. But the Commissioner of Police does not risk relying solely on competitive examinations: he sees the danger that a good examinee may not always be the best officer, and vice versa. No constable may therefore sit for the examination unless he is certified by his superintendent as in every way fit for promotion. It would seem that this condition will detract severely from the purely competitive character of the process, but it is too soon yet to say whether it is working fairly or, perhaps more important, is thought by the force to be working fairly.

Promotion Rates

Promotion rates have, of course, varied from time to time and in different types of force, but, on the whole, they have been very slow. Thus of the entrants to all forces in Great Britain from 1919 to 1921 who were still in the police after $24\frac{1}{2}$ years, 67 per cent. were still in the rank of constable. Of the remaining 33 per cent. who had been promoted to sergeant or above, 14 per cent. were inspectors or above, and 2 per cent. were superintendents or above. Thus, if a man stayed in the police for $24\frac{1}{2}$ years, he had a 1 in 3 chance of becoming a sergeant or above by the end of that time, a 1 in 7 chance of becoming an inspector or above, and a slightly better than 1 in 50 chance of becoming a superintendent or above. These rates give the chance of promotion for all entrants. The possibility of promotion has, however, depended on passing the qualifying examinations. After $24\frac{1}{2}$ years from the date of entry, 51 per cent. of the men still in the police had passed the examinations qualifying for promotion to sergeant, and, of those who had qualified, 65 per cent. had been promoted to the rank of sergeant or above. Among the sergeants, three in every five who were qualified for promotion were promoted to inspector before completing $24\frac{1}{2}$ years' service. Amongst the entrants to the police between 1919 and 1921, a small number of constables were promoted to sergeant after as few as six or seven years, but some had to wait for 20 years or more. The average time spent as constable before promotion was 13·2 years. Promotions to inspector occurred generally after 15 to 20 years' service.

In 1947, 77 per cent. of the police were constables, 16 per cent. sergeants, 5½ per cent. inspectors, and 1½ per cent. superintendents or above. The percentages in the ranks above constable were higher in 1947 than in 1927 or in 1937: 23 per cent. in 1947 as compared with 18 per cent. in 1927 and 1937, but there do not seem to be any good grounds for thinking that the rank structure of the police will alter appreciably during the next decade or so. There may be alterations in the factors permanently affecting promotion, but they are not likely to be very substantial. This is important: it means that it will always be impossible for at least half and probably two-thirds of constables to be promoted, and incentives other than promotion should be found to keep men happy and keen as constables. What form these should take, i.e. more increments of pay, bonuses for outstanding work, special privileges, etc., need not concern us here. What is important is that a constable's life should be thought of as a career in itself and that promotion should not be every constable's aim. A solution along these lines would be far more satisfactory than any attempt to improve promotion prospects by requiring, as is sometimes suggested, all police officers above a certain rank, e.g. constable, to retire after 30 years' service regardless of their age, capacities and desires. Compulsory retirement at certain ages is, of course, the rule, but to go beyond this would be wasteful of the services of useful men.

The Origins of Chief Constables

The only exception to the practice of appointing policemen to the rank of constable is in the case of Chief Constables and assistant Chief Constables. In the 19th century a large number, probably the majority, of county Chief Constables were appointed to their posts from outside the police service—not infrequently they were retired members of the armed forces. The practice was less common in the case of borough Chief Constables. Between the two world wars the practice of appointing men from outside the police declined, but it did not altogether cease. Figures for the whole period are not available, but the following give some indication of what took place. From 1924 to 1937, 154 Chief Constables were appointed to provincial forces in England and Wales. Of these, 131, or 85 per cent., had previous police experience in Great Britain. In most cases this will mean that they had started their service in the rank

of constable, but some of the 131 had served only as Chief
Constables. Of the remaining 23, or 15 per cent., who had no
previous police experience in Great Britain, 16 had police
experience overseas, but probably not in the lower ranks, and
seven had no previous police experience at all. Since the second
world war, the proportion appointed from outside the police has
remained about the same: thus in 1947 and 1948, out of 30 appointments, seven had had virtually no experience in the lower ranks.

It is therefore wrong, though not uncommon, to think that the
majority of Chief Constables are to-day ex-service officers with no
previous police experience. In the case of the borough forces, it is
very rare indeed for someone other than a policeman to be appointed Chief Constable; but in the county forces there is still a sprink-
ling of Chief Constables who have had no experience in the ranks
of the police. The difference between the practice in counties and
boroughs can probably be accounted for by the different social
origins and preferences of members of Standing Joint Committees
and Watch Committees.

It seems to the outsider strange that the police service should
know nothing between the two extremes of (*a*) starting all men at
the bottom and making them work their way slowly up the ladder,
and (*b*) appointing men to the highest posts (Chief Constable and
occasionally assistant Chief Constable) in middle age with no
experience of the police in any rank. The practice of filling all posts
except the very highest by promotion from the lower ranks originated with Peel's rule for the Metropolitan force. He was extremely
anxious to prevent jobbery and improper pressure, political and
personal, in the building up of the new force, and the decision was
undoubtedly right at the time. No definite rule to the same effect
was made for provincial forces, though the Home Secretary's rules
of 1857 for county forces contain the following curious passage:
'When vacancies occur in the office of superintendent, inspector or
sergeant, it is desirable that encouragement should be given to
meritorious men serving in the subordinate stations, by their promotion to the higher stations when they are qualified.' Whether
because of this rule or because they were influenced by the Metropolitan practice, almost all appointments to provincial forces in the
19th century, except in the case of Chief Constables, were in the
rank of constable from which promotion was slow and uncertain.

The ultimate effect of this effort to be egalitarian was just the opposite of what was intended: it was found that the man who was willing to start and remain for many years as a constable for a small wage was seldom suitable to become a Chief Constable, lacking as he usually did education and administrative capacity, and there was, therefore, a tendency for the very top posts to be filled from outside the police. This was by no means altogether satisfactory, apart from the fact that it had naturally a discouraging effect on the lower ranks. In the worst cases the posts of Chief Constable were regarded as comfortable sinecures into which ex-service officers could retire in middle life and fish and shoot with the county gentry. The answer to the dilemma would have been either to bring in to the middle ranks of the police young men who by their education, personality and administrative ability showed promise of being able to fill some of the higher posts later on, or greatly to speed up the promotion of the ablest men. It was obvious that no educated young man would join the police whilst he had no chance of promotion and little responsibility for such a very long period. It was these considerations which led the Government at the suggestion of Lord Trenchard to set up the Hendon Police College in 1933.

The Hendon Experiment and the New Police College

Admission to the Hendon Police College was partly by competitive examination, partly by selection. The students were all young men; about three-quarters of them had had experience— often very brief—in the lowest ranks of the Metropolitan police force, and about one-quarter came from outside, usually from school or university. On passing out, after one to two years' training, they were given the rank of inspector in the Metropolitan police force. The aim was to send to the college promising men when they were still sufficiently young to learn quickly and to train them to fill responsible posts in the police.

A great deal of controversy has raged round this scheme. The Police Federation were opposed to it from the start. They thought that the best training for the higher posts was long service starting from the bottom and moving slowly up the ladder; they were naturally hostile to men being brought in from outside and, after training, going straight into positions of responsibility, as this inevitably decreased the chances of promotion of those in the lower ranks, even though a short-service scheme for the Metropolitan police was introduced at the same time; they also feared that the selection of men from the force would give scope for favouritism. More generally it was said by other critics that the Government was aiming at militarising the police and at creating an 'officer class'. In fact the aims of the Government were simply to remove the absurdity of a public profession which was unable to produce its own higher officers, and to improve the efficiency of the force. It was unfortunate for the popularity of the scheme that Lord Trenchard brought some students in from outside, largely from public schools, with no previous police experience, and that he did not confine it to men from the ranks of the police, but he certainly saw what was wrong with the service and tackled the problem in a bold and far-sighted way. It is difficult to draw any conclusions about the college from the subsequent careers of its students, but it is worth noting that several of them have become Chief Constables in provincial forces. Another criticism made of the college was that it was not open to provincial police officers. The Government started with a Metropolitan police college because it seemed most unlikely that support would be received for a national one, an attempt to establish one a few years earlier having failed. A few provincial policemen were in fact admitted to the college, but this part of the scheme was not very successful.

The Hendon Police College was closed on the outbreak of war in 1939 and has not been reopened. Instead the Government set up in 1947 a National Police College on rather different lines. In doing this, they were advised by a committee which consisted overwhelmingly of senior police officials, who appear to have paid little or no attention to the Hendon experiment, except that they were aware of its unpopularity. The purpose of the new college is to provide training for the middle and higher ranks of the police, by broadening their outlook, increasing their knowledge and stimulating their interest. It will normally be open only to sergeants who have passed the examination for inspector, and to the ranks above sergeant. It follows that students will normally be at least 27 years old, and that the average age will probably be 35 to 40. The Government also proposes that a small number of constables who have passed the qualifying examinations to sergeant and inspector should be admitted with the Home Secretary's approval.

While this plan may help to prepare the best of existing sergeants for higher responsibility and give a fillip to the higher ranks, it will do little or nothing to attract to the police young men with ambition who not unreasonably will not be prepared to stay in the lower ranks for many years. Promotion prospects must, as we have seen, remain poor, and the ordinary course of a policeman's career does not fit him for the higher, or often for the intermediate, ranks. It is all the more important that able men should enter the police, as they enter other professions, the armed forces, and business, in the knowledge that after a few years in the lower ranks they have a fair chance of selection for more responsible and interesting work. The Government have admitted that Hendon brought in good men who might otherwise not have joined the service, but they were not prepared to go against the wishes of the rank and file of the police, and indeed of the higher officers. The rank and file are terrified of favouritism, which is perhaps inevitable in a system in which promotion is in the hands of the local chief or police authority and there is no one to whom an appeal can be made against their decision. It may have been a wise short-term policy not to have risked causing considerable discontent in the police, but as a long-term policy it would undoubtedly have been better to have adopted a scheme which would have given able policemen a chance of promotion far earlier and quicker than they have now. Apart from anything else this should have helped to attract good recruits to the service. At present, for instance, practically no university graduate ever thinks of joining the police; but the service undoubtedly needs the trained minds of some graduates. It is not suggested here that policemen should not start at the bottom and spend a few years on practical police work: this is desirable (though the case for it is by no means as clear as many policemen think), if only because the work at the bottom is so very different from the work at the top, which is not so in some occupations; but it is suggested that brilliant men will not enter, or if they enter remain in, the service unless their prospects are greatly improved.

During the first year of its existence, the average age of those attending the 'junior' course at the college, which lasts six months, was 37, and there was no student under 30. The Federation does not regard this as too high, but the Home Secretary is anxious that whilst the elderly are not excluded, some younger men shall be included. Selection for the college is made entirely by the Chief Officer or police authority within the quota of vacancies allocated to them, which gives them considerable responsibility. There has been no change in the system of promotion as a result of the institution of the college: attendance at the college does not give a man a right to promotion, but the number of students attending the junior courses is fixed in the light of the estimated number of promotions each year, and it seems probable that men who have been to the college will be more likely to be promoted than those who have not, though there may, of course, be those who would have been promoted anyway. About one-third of the curriculum is concerned with general matters, such as our system of government, current affairs and 'English', and about two-thirds with police practice, administration and law. Besides including formal lectures, instruction is by the discussion method and practical exercises. A great deal of emphasis is laid on getting the students to think for themselves and to exchange their experience and knowledge. It may be doubted whether it is necessary or desirable to foster tradition and 'esprit de corps' quite as much as is done, but undoubtedly the curriculum is on the right lines and in spite of the emphasis on tradition, the staff show a healthy desire to experiment with teaching methods.

Ultimate control of the college is vested in a Board of Governors composed of eight members nominated by the local authority associations (the nominees being mostly or all members of police authorities) and eight members nominated by the Home Secretary (who are all police officers except a chairman from the Home Office). The day-to-day administration of the college is in the hands of a committee which is composed of police officers, an Inspector of Constabulary and a member of his staff. This committee is the really effective body, though in form it only advises the Commandant and the Board of Governors. The machinery seems to be working reasonably well, though there might be some advantage in putting on these bodies one or two persons who are not connected with the police. The service tends to be a 'closed shop' and it might benefit by more contact with outsiders, e.g. in the case of the college, people with experience of adult education generally or those concerned with training schemes for other professions. But on the whole the college is undoubtedly a success and is doing the best it can given the framework within which it has to act. It is, however, to be hoped that this framework will gradually be widened so that younger men will be sent to the college, thus encouraging able people to join the police and enabling the higher posts (including that of Commissioner of Police of the Metropolis) to be filled from serving policemen.

CHAPTER IX

Scotland

Note: In this chapter, for the sake of brevity, the terms 'England' and 'English' are used throughout to mean 'England and Wales' and 'English and Welsh'.

THE general structure of Scottish police organisation is, broadly speaking, similar to the English. North as well as south of the border, there are a number of independent police forces, varying considerably in size, controlled by local police authorities, and the Secretary of State for Scotland has responsibilities for police administration in Scotland similar to those possessed by the Home Secretary for the provincial police of England. The fact that Scottish law is in many respects different from English law has not resulted in different structures in the police services of the two countries, and just as local government has evolved on *broadly* similar lines in Scotland and England, if both are compared with many foreign countries, so the organisation and control of the police is in the main similar.

History

Scottish patriots claim that police forces on the new, reformed model were set up in some towns in Scotland before the Metropolitan police force was formed in 1829. It is true that at the beginning of the 19th century several Scottish towns secured local Acts of Parliament to enable them to improve their paving, cleansing, watching and lighting—as indeed did many English towns. Thus Glasgow secured such an Act in 1800, Edinburgh in 1805, Paisley in 1806, and Greenock in 1810. These Acts no doubt resulted in some, and often considerable, improvement in the policing of the towns concerned, but the problem to be tackled was small compared with the problem of policing London, and it seems improbable that the changes made were as drastic.

The first general police Act for Scottish towns was passed in

1833; it enabled the larger burghs to elect Commissioners who could appoint police officers and make rules for watching. In 1847 and 1850, the Act was extended to smaller towns, but each locality was still left free to decide whether or not to adopt the Act and to set up a police force, with the result that progress varied from place to place. Scottish burghs were not required by Act of Parliament to establish police forces until 1892—whereas the corresponding date for England was 1835—but there was not so much difference in the progress of police organisation in the two countries as these dates would suggest, as most Scottish burghs acted before they were compelled to by statute.

Whatever conclusion is reached as to the rival claims of Scottish burghs and London to be the first in the field with a 'new model' police force, there seems little doubt that the rural areas of Scotland were, in the 19th century, not in advance of those of England in this matter. The freeholders had had power since 1724 to levy 'rogue money' to defray the cost of apprehending and prosecuting criminals, but, as in England, it was not until 1839 that power was given to set up a constabulary force on a county basis. An Act of that year gave authority to maintain a police force in each county to Commissioners of Supply; these were local landowners, originally appointed to levy the land tax who had had imposed on them various administrative duties corresponding to those exercised in England by justices of the peace. The Act resulted in some improvement, but it was not adopted everywhere and it gave the Secretary of State fewer powers of control over the Commissioners of Supply than he was given over the justices of the peace by the English County Police Act of 1839.

In 1857, the Police (Scotland) Act, which was modelled closely on the English County and Borough Police Act of 1856, *required* Commissioners of Supply to establish a police force in each county, and placed the administration of each force under Police Committees composed of the Commissioners, the Lord Lieutenant, the Sheriff and the magistrates of certain burghs. The Act authorised the inspection of burgh and county forces and provided for the payment of a Government grant up to one-quarter of the cost of the pay and clothing of the police, where efficient. The Secretary of State was authorised to make rules for the government, pay, etc., of the county police, but he did not obtain similar powers over the

burgh police until 1892. Yet this was in advance of the corresponding date for England, which was 1919.

The Scottish inspector found from the start very much the
same defects as his colleagues in England, especially lock-ups unfit
for any human being, shocking living quarters for the lower ranks,
too few policemen and too many small separate forces which did
not co-operate. The position in this respect was indeed worse than
in England where forces outside London have on an average
always been, and still are, 75 to 100 per cent. larger than in Scotland.
In 1889 there were 16 forces in Scotland with less than 10 men each,
and 31 with less than 20. The Inspector constantly pressed for
legislation to abolish the smaller forces, but apart from the elimination of forces in three burghs with less than 7,000 inhabitants by the
Local Government (Scotland) Act, 1889, no Scottish forces were
compulsorily amalgamated until 1929. In 1919 there were as many
(24) forces with less than 25 men in Scotland as in England. The
Desborough Committee of that year recommended that all separate
police forces in burghs with less than 50,000 inhabitants should be
merged in the county force, which would have reduced the number
of forces by one-third—to about 40 forces. Nothing so drastic was
done, but a start was made in 1929 when, by the Local Government
(Scotland) Act of that year, eight burgh forces were abolished and
two groups of two county forces were combined. The matter was
thoroughly examined again by the Police Consolidation (Scotland)
Committee in 1933. The Committee was impressed by the usual
arguments, but especially by the case for economy, and in spite of
the well-known opposition of small police authorities, made an
even more drastic recommendation, namely, the reduction of the
then 48 forces to 14 during the ensuing seven years, by compulsion
if necessary; but the Government apparently thought it had gone
in 1929 as far as it should and did not implement this recommendation.

The figures on page 171 show how the number of Scottish forces
has been gradually reduced and how efficiency has improved.

During the 19th century, until 1885, when the Scottish Office
was set up, the Home Secretary was advised on Scottish matters
by the Lord Advocate, and on the whole the standard set in London
for the policing of Scotland, particularly as regards numbers, seems
to have been rather lower than for England, partly no doubt out of

Year	No. of police forces	Forces certified inefficient
1859 . . .	89	40
1865 . . .	84	18
1871 . . .	68	7
1886 . . .	69	4
1900 . . .	64	—
1910 . . .	63	2
1920 . . .	59	—
1930 . . .	49	—
1939 . . .	48	—
1946 . . .	49	—
1949 . . .	36	—

a diplomatic respect for the feelings of the Scottish people. Nevertheless, as in England, the number of policemen employed and the proportion of police to population increased steadily as the following figures show:

Year	Total police strength	Population per police officer
1859 . . .	2,460	1,108
1871 . . .	3,000	1,001
1886 . . .	3,840	945 (estimate)
1900 . . .	4,920	887
1910 . . .	5,620	856
1918 . . .	5,950	819
1921 . . .	6,490	757
1931 . . .	6,560	732
1939 . . .	7,010	690
1948 . . .	7,080	731

Changes have also been made in the constitution of the bodies responsible for the control of the police. In 1889, when County Councils were set up in Scotland, County Councillors were as in England given some, but not complete, responsibility for the police, the powers of the Commissioners of Supply being transferred to Standing Joint Committees of seven County Councillors and seven Commissioners of Supply who were retained for this purpose alone; but in 1929 a break with the English system was made: Standing Joint Committees were abolished and the County Council was made the police authority for county forces. The Acts governing the policing of towns, except the five remaining with local Acts, were consolidated and amplified by the important Burgh Police (Scotland) Act of 1892, and in 1900 such Commissioners as still retained police powers lost them to Town Councils. The five towns which are still policed under local Acts are Glasgow, Edinburgh, Dundee, Aberdeen and Greenock.

In 1919 the Scottish police system was suffering from the same difficulties as the English: superannuation was no longer a serious grievance as it had been during the 19th century, but pay and other conditions of service were generally poor and varied widely from force to force; there was considerable discontent and a police union existed. There were, however, no strikes. The reforms of 1919–1921 were applied to Scotland as well as to England: the Secretary for Scotland was given power to regulate the pay and conditions of service of the Scottish police, and a Scottish Police Council and Police Federation were established. In many ways, however, the Scottish police system lagged behind the English and exhibited in extreme form the weaknesses of British police organisation. This was no doubt due to geographical conditions and to the relative poverty of Scotland. Thus between the wars the Inspectors reported that individual forces tended to forget that they were units in the Scottish police service; that there was not sufficient co-operation in the detection of crime; that there were grave difficulties in training and promotion in the smaller forces; and that many forces were backward technically: for instance, the *Scottish Police Gazette*, in which the names of all wanted persons are circulated, was not started until 1934 (though it had been recommended by the Inspectors since 1860), and some police stations were still without telephones in 1937. Moreover Chief Constables did not meet regularly in district conferences until 1939—over 20 years after the practice had started in England.

The war and post-war years have seen much the same developments in Scotland as in England: a more positive attitude both at the centre and locally has taken the place of the pre-war *laissez faire* spirit. All recruits have to be trained; there are more opportunities for police officers interested in the same problems to meet each other; a new system of policing which has rightly attracted considerable attention has been introduced in Aberdeen; and above all since the war the number of forces has been substantially reduced.

No Scottish forces were amalgamated under the Defence Regulations, but they did not escape post-war consolidations. The case for amalgamations was certainly strong: of the 49 separate Scottish forces which existed in 1945, 20 had a strength of less than 50, and 11 of less than 30.

The Police (Scotland) Act, 1946, did not, as its English counterpart did, abolish any police forces outright; but it gave power to any two or more police authorities, whether county or burghal, to arrange, subject to the approval of the Secretary of State, for the amalgamation of their police areas and police forces, and for the maintenance and administration of the combined police force by a Joint Police Committee consisting of representatives of the police authorities concerned. It also gave the Secretary of State power to effect compulsory amalgamations. There are the same safeguards as in the English Act: an independent enquiry must be held if required, and the scheme must be laid before Parliament; but there is no limit of population beyond which mergers cannot be effected without the consent of the police authorities concerned.

By 1949, nine amalgamation schemes had been made, all voluntary in form, but some not in fact, as many authorities were warned that if no scheme were submitted a compulsory order would be made. These schemes will reduce the number of Scottish forces from 49 to 33; some combine as many as four forces together. Most of the joint authorities so formed are not combined for any purposes other than police, and though, as in England, there are certain drawbacks to such *ad hoc* authorities, from the purely police point of view there is clear gain. The schemes are on broadly the same lines as the English ones: each old police authority appoints a prescribed number of its members to the new joint authority; and the joint authority cannot itself levy a rate, but has power to call on each constituent authority for its contribution calculated in certain ways which vary from scheme to scheme. Unlike the English, the Scottish schemes, perhaps wisely, provide how differences between participating authorities shall be settled: normally the Sheriff or the Secretary of State is to act as arbitrator. The Secretary of State has not announced the target (if any) to which he is working, but it seems probable that he will reduce the number of forces in Scotland further still, even if not to the 14 recommended by the Committee of 1933.

Present Organisation of the Scottish Police and Differences from England

The local authorities in charge of the Scottish police are therefore County Councils, Town Councils and joint *ad hoc* committees representing these Councils. Of the 33 County Councils in Scotland in 1950, only nine maintain separate police forces of their own; the remaining 24 have combined with other counties or with towns to maintain joint forces, of which there are 13.

Amongst the towns, the four counties of cities, Edinburgh, Glasgow, Aberdeen and Dundee, which correspond to English county boroughs, maintain their own police forces; and of the 20 large burghs, half maintain separate forces. No small burgh has had a force since 1929, except Lerwick which had a force of its own until the Act of 1857 was applied to Zetland in 1940. The forces vary greatly in size from 2,200 (Glasgow) to 12 (Zetland); there is only one other (Edinburgh) with over 500 members; of the remainder, five are in the 250 to 500 range, 13 in the 100 to 250 range and 16 have less than 100 members.

Since 1885, when the office of Secretary for Scotland was instituted, the powers of the Secretary of State in relation to the Scottish police have been exercised not by the Home Secretary, but by the Secretary for Scotland (who was promoted to Secretary of State in 1926), but on all main issues they pursue the same policy. One or two subjects affecting the work of the police, e.g. the control of aliens, are, by arrangement, dealt with by the Home Office throughout Great Britain, and there is not a separate inspectorate for policewomen, but otherwise the Scottish and English police are separately administered. There is, however, when necessary, close contact between the Home Office and Scottish Home Department. It is, indeed, specifically provided in the Police Act, 1919—in terms now unusual in a statute—that in making police regulations under the Act, the Home Secretary and the Secretary for Scotland 'shall act in consultation with one another'.

In the autumn of 1949, the Scottish police numbered 6,900, of whom 120 were women. Police authorities were authorised to employ 7,450. This gives an overall average of 694 inhabitants for each authorised police officer and 750 inhabitants for each actual police officer. The corresponding figures for England were lower:

600 and 720. The ratio naturally varies considerably from place to place—from over 1,000 inhabitants per policeman in several counties to 475 in Glasgow. The average for rural areas is 60 per cent. higher than the average for towns.

Policewomen were first employed in Scotland at about the same time as in England. The following figures show how, as in England, it is only recently that their numbers have increased substantially.

Year	Policewomen employed	Police authorities	
		Employing women	Not employing women
1921 . .	14	3	56
1930 . .	17	5	44
1939 . .	37	11	37
1949 . .	123	26	10

In Scotland, as in England, every police officer, whatever his rank, holds the office of constable, which has existed for many centuries, but the oath taken on appointment is slightly different: in Scotland he does not swear that he will 'serve the King in the office of constable', as in England, but that he will 'faithfully discharge the duties of the office of constable'. His status, which has, as in England, been the subject of judicial decisions (indeed earlier ones) is, however, substantially the same: he is not a servant of the police authority, but a ministerial officer of the Crown, a public servant, 'a joint agent with various authorities in securing the preservation of order, and entrusted both with statutory and common law powers for that purpose.' (*Simpson* v. *Dundee Corporation*, 1928, S.N.)

There are special constables in Scotland as in England, but the purposes for which they can, under statute, be employed (aiding the police 'on occasions of emergency, and for suppressing or preventing tumult or riot') are more restricted than in England (the preservation of the public peace and the protection of the inhabitants and the security of property).

There are, however, some important differences in the organisation of the police in Scotland and England. In the first place, in

Scotland there is no force for which the Secretary of State is the police authority, as the Home Secretary is for the Metropolitan police force. Secondly, there are differences in the constitution and powers of police authorities. In counties, as we have seen, the police authority is the County Council and not, like its English counterpart, composed half of justices of the peace. In determining whether to make County Councils the police authorities in counties in England, the experience of Scotland would, of course, be material, but unfortunately no comparative survey of the working of the two systems has been made. The County Council in Scotland is required by statute to appoint a Police Committee to which all police matters unless urgent must be referred, but this Committee is not the police authority. A County Council may not delegate its police powers to burgh or district councils, but County Councils contain representatives of all burghs which are policed by the county force, whereas in England no town which is not of county borough status has a representative on the county police authority. In the towns, the police authority is the Town Council; the Council may if it wishes form a Police Committee, but this Committee is not, like the English Watch Committee, the police authority.

Police authorities in Scotland are, as in England, primarily responsible for maintaining efficient police forces in their areas: they fix the size of their force and the numbers in the various ranks, subject to the approval of the Secretary of State, and they provide houses, cells, equipment, etc. Subject to the approval of the Secretary of State, they appoint the Chief Constable, except in Glasgow, where the appointment is made by the magistrates and Sheriff, and in Aberdeen, where it is made by the police authority (Town Council) and Sheriff Principal. But there is a difference between the powers of control over the force of burgh police authorities in Scotland and those of Watch Committees in England. In Scotland the Town Council does not possess the legal power to appoint, promote or dismiss members of the force below the rank of Chief Constable; these powers are, with a few minor exceptions, vested in the Chief Constable. The chief exceptions are as follows: in Glasgow the Magistrates' Committee is the disciplinary authority for members of the force above the rank of inspector, and in most towns the Chief Constable's selection of a deputy needs the approval of the Magistrates. Generally speaking, however, Scottish burgh

Chief Constables do not have to share with anyone else their authority in matters of internal administration, as borough Chief Constables have to in England, and the position is therefore more satisfactory in Scotland. In Scottish county forces, on the other hand, the police authority has certain powers not possessed by county police authorities in England: the Chief Constable's appointments to the force are subject to the authority's approval. It is very rare, if not unknown, for an authority to refuse to approve the Chief Constable's choice, but the legal right is theirs and it would seem that the law should be made to conform to the practice. Promotions are in county forces made by the Chief Constable alone, and he is the sole disciplinary authority.

There is also an important difference (as was mentioned in chapter IV) between the position of the Scottish and English police in regard to the prosecution of offenders. In Scotland the police are investigators, but not, except to a limited extent, prosecutors: the duty to prosecute and to decide whether or not to prosecute in most criminal cases rests with legal officers of the Crown—the Lord Advocate and his subordinates. It is therefore, at any rate theoretically, possible to secure more uniformity in the enforcement of the law in Scotland than in England; whether in fact it is more uniformly enforced it is difficult to say, and in any event it is not easy, in determining this question, to isolate the factor of the prosecuting agent from other factors such as differences in legal procedure. The respective spheres of the police and of the Crown prosecutors in the investigation of crimes have not always been clear, and in the past a solution to these difficulties has sometimes been sought by appointing a police officer to the Crown prosecutor's staff; this is no longer the practice, but the system, nevertheless, now works smoothly.

The following further differences are also worth mentioning. (1) In Scotland no person without previous police experience of at least five years may be appointed Chief Constable. This has been the rule since 1920. As nearly all appointments are made to the rank of constable, the result is that almost without exception Scottish Chief Constables have risen from the ranks and one does not find, as in England, retired ex-service men as Chief Constables. (2) The rate of wastage amongst policemen in Scotland is lower than in England, and as recruitment is reasonably satisfactory, the overall percentage deficiency in strength is also much lower. The most probable explanation of these differences is that the level of unemployment in Scotland is higher than in any other part of Great Britain except Wales. (3) Owing to difficulty in finding suitable premises for a Government training centre, recruit training had for a time after the war to be provided by Glasgow, Edinburgh, and Aberdeen. A central residential training school for recruits has now, however, been established, the machinery for management being similar to the English. It is intended to establish a police college in Scotland, but suitable premises have not yet been found, and apart from sending a few police officers to the English college, there is at present no higher training of the Scottish police. (4) Promotion prospects are less good in Scotland than in England, though a higher percentage of policemen pass the qualifying examinations, which is no doubt due to the higher level of general education in Scotland.

The Police (Appeals) Acts, which give police officers a right to appeal to the Secretary of State in the more serious type of disciplinary case, apply to Scotland as to England, the only material difference being that an enquiry in a Scottish case must be held by the Sheriff Principal, whereas in England an enquiry is held by an *ad hoc* tribunal appointed by the Home Secretary. A higher proportion of appeals has been allowed in Scotland than in England, but it is not possible to account for this on the information available.

The rate of Exchequer grant in aid of expenditure on the police is, as in England, 50 per cent., but the grant in Scotland has, as has been seen, since 1947 been given a permanent statutory basis. It is improbable, however, that this will involve any change in the type of expenditure passed for grant. The total cost of the Scottish police in the financial year 1949–1950 was £4,730,000; Government grant amounted to £2,345,000; the average cost per police officer was £682 as compared with £791 in England. The total cost of the Scottish police in 1950–1951 is estimated as £5,256,000. This is a far cry from those days early in the 18th century when in an Act of Parliament passed 'for more effectual disarming the Highlands in that part of Great Britain called Scotland' it was recited that there was 'want of a sufficient fund for defraying the charges of apprehending criminals in North Britain and of subsisting them when apprehended, until prosecution', and one can but hope that with the assistance of these £5 million, fewer criminals now 'escape the punishment due to their offences' (11 Geo. 1, ch. 26).

Books

Very little has been written about the Scottish police; the best account of its historical development will be found in the 'Encyclopædia of Scottish Laws', and the first two chapters of James Mill's 'The Scottish Police' (1944) are of general interest.

CHAPTER X

Conclusions

'THE police are one of our British institutions in which as a nation
we take most pride, and on the whole we can claim that our police
force yields to none and is, we believe, superior to all in efficiency,
and in what is the first condition of efficiency, honesty'. (Sir Herbert
Samuel, 1937.) Claims of this kind are not infrequently made about
the British police. Other writers and speakers have stressed the good
relations which exist between the police and the public; and we
constantly pride ourselves on the fact that there is no 'police state'
here. This is not the place to consider whether the British police are
efficient or honest, but which features in our system of organisation
are valuable, why relations between the police and the public are
on the whole good, and how we differ from 'police states'.

Local Control

The local basis of British police organisation is usually regarded
as its most characteristic and valuable feature. The existence of a
large number of independent forces and local police authorities is
said to be one of our safeguards against tyranny and the 'police
state'. It is also claimed that because the members of each force are
usually recruited locally, the people they police have confidence in
them. There is some truth—in fact a good deal of truth—in these
contentions. Local control of the police is undoubtedly a great
safeguard against tyranny. Suppose the Secretary of State ordered
Chief Constables to take some action for which there was no legal
authority: some of them might do it on the ground that they had
received an order from the highest quarters, relying on the Government to back them up in the event of subsequent difficulties; but
others might well refuse to obey the Secretary of State's order
knowing that there was nothing he could do about their defiance. He
could not bring an action against them e.g. for refusal to obey a
lawful order; he could not demote or dismiss them, for a Chief
Constable is appointed by the local police authority, subject only to

CONCLUSIONS   181

the initial approval of the Secretary of State. If Chief Constables were appointed by the Government and removable by it at will, the situation would be very different.

There is also a good deal to be said for local recruitment. There are still variations in customs and characteristics from one part of the country to another even in 20th-century Britain, and it is desirable that the police should understand these differences. This is more important than in the case of some other services such as e.g. the post office. In some cases a thorough understanding of the peculiarities of a locality may enable the police to enforce a law or may save them from incurring ridicule by trying to do so. On the other hand, there are, of course, some drawbacks to local recruitment: a policeman may be too intimately connected with a neighbourhood for him to be able to be as detached and impartial as he should be. Perhaps the ideal is for him to come from a neighbouring district. In any event the police authority will be composed of local people: this is all the more necessary to-day when the Chief Constable is often not a local man as he was usually in the past.

But it is possible to exaggerate the benefits of our system of independent, locally controlled forces and to forget its drawbacks. The most important of these will have become apparent from what has been said in earlier chapters. One is the difficulty in getting 165 forces to co-operate with one another in their work. Arrangements for sending reinforcements from one force to another are certainly far better than they were 30 or even 10 years ago, but mutual aid is likely to remain one of the weaker features of the system. Difficulties also result from the fact that the forces do not all use the same system in their criminal work. A good deal of standardisation has been introduced during the last 15 years, but here again there is probably still room for improvement, and it is a weakness which is almost bound to arise with our police system. There are other weaknesses such as the backwardness of some forces on the technical side, but these are not a result of their independence so much as of their size. One can envisage a system—in fact we now seem to be working towards it—where there are a number of independent forces, but big enough to carry the necessary technical equipment and experts, supplemented by certain centrally run services. The difficulty in the past has been that ever since our modern police system started in the 19th century, there have been quite a large number of forces which were too small to develop or support the necessary technical services.

It must also be remembered that just as the Secretary of State cannot direct provincial Chief Constables to interfere improperly with our liberties, so he can do little to prevent them doing so. This is the price we pay for our 'non-police state'. Thus if the police employ methods of which many people disapprove such as acting as *agents provocateurs*, or if they persecute members of a political party by raiding their houses, or breaking up or preventing their meetings, the Secretary of State has no power to instruct the Chief Constable concerned to cease from these practices however much he disapproves of them. He may, of course, put pressure on the Chief Constable in an unofficial way; this will probably depend on the personalities involved and on the state of public opinion; but he has no simple remedy at hand. When things like this happen, there will always be people who will ask that the Government should instruct the police to behave differently, but it will usually reply that it has no power to interfere with the provincial police. Theoretically the people who object can bring pressure to bear on their representatives on the local police authority and ask that they should ensure that the force behaves differently, but there are various difficulties in the way of doing this: most police authorities are chary of interfering with the Chief Constable's executive acts, and in the counties especially the police authority does not meet sufficiently often for it to be able to take effective action in matters of this kind. Another remedy which is open to those who are aggrieved by the practices of the police is to bring an action against the officers directly concerned with a view to getting their activities condemned in the courts, and perhaps personal damages. The British courts are normally keen guardians of our liberties, and even *obiter dicta* from a court on the activities of the police are usually effective in making them for a time respect public opinion in these matters. The fact remains that instances have occurred where the Chief Constable has been able to ride his particular hobby horse without adequate restraints, e.g. in the internment of harmless enemy aliens during the war. Occurrences of this kind point to the importance of the greatest care being taken in the selection of Chief Constables.

A Chief Constable and a police authority have also a certain amount of power over the lives and welfare of members of their force. In the past some of them imposed restrictions which interfered unnecessarily with the private lives of policemen—e.g. restrictions on marrying, on activities during leave or on rest days. The scope for this kind of despotism, some of it benevolent, has recently been reduced, but Chief Constables and police authorities, nevertheless, retain a certain discretion to determine local conditions of service.

The risks we run in giving responsibility to police authorities are, of course, intrinsic to any system of self-government. The difficulty is that borough police authorities in England and Wales have been given powers and duties which are not suitable for any committee, i.e. disciplinary powers, and powers to appoint and promote members of the force. The Secretary of State can, of course, bring pressure on a police authority, through the Exchequer grant, in a way which he cannot on a Chief Constable, but the harm, such as it is, is usually done before he can intervene. Attention was drawn in an earlier chapter to deficiencies in the arrangements for investigating allegations against Chief Constables.

Nationalisation

We can perhaps better assess the value of our present police organisation if we consider the main alternative to it: a nationalised system. If the police were administered on the same lines as the fire service during the second world war, local police authorities would disappear, their functions being taken over by Chief Constables or more often by the Secretary of State. In spite of all the shortcomings of local police authorities, this would undoubtedly be a change for the worse since it would make it easier for the Government to interfere with our political and personal liberties. It would also enable the Government to secure more uniformity in the enforcement of the law in so far as this can be secured by the prosecuting authority. This is not the place to discuss whether there should be a more uniform policy in prosecuting; it is sufficient here to point out that if the police were nationalised, the Secretary of State would probably issue directions rather than advice on such matters, and Chief Constables would obey them.

From the purely technical point of view, nationalisation would probably result in increased efficiency, provided the machine were not so big that it became cumbrous and Whitehall had to be referred to before anything was done. If the machine functioned properly it should be possible to improve the general standard of police work, particularly the prevention and detection of crime by such things as the most complete exchange of information, the abolition of inter-force jealousies, the complete standardisation of criminal records, etc. It would be easier to improve the weak spots in the service: for example, the possession of certain equipment would not be dependent on the wealth of a particular police area. There would undoubtedly be advantages in nationalisation from this point of view, especially as the weakness of one force has repercussions outside its own area.

From the point of view of the police themselves, nationalisation would probably make little difference so far as pay and most of their conditions of service were concerned, as these are already uniform throughout the country. It would probably mean the disappearance of certain local variations in minor conditions of service, which would not be very significant. More important would be the effect on promotion. If the same ratio of higher to lower ranks were maintained, promotion, taking the service as a whole, would not be any faster or slower, but it should mean less irregularity in the speed of promotion of people with similar ability and claims to rise. Under the present system promotion chances vary from force to force according to various circumstances, and it is very difficult to get transferred from one force to another. This falls hardly on men who may have some good reason for wishing to move to another force. It is possible, of course, that promotion in a nationalised force would present problems of the same kind, only on a bigger scale, as are presented by the Metropolitan force; but it should not be impossible to devise a satisfactory system. If transfers from one area to another were made regardless of the men's wishes, there might well be discontent, and this would no doubt be a matter on which the Federation would demand certain guarantees.

Nationalisation of the British police has seldom been advocated. It has never been on the programme of any of the main political parties, and among police officers there have only been a few lone voices raised in its favour, usually from senior officers in the Metropolitan police force. When it is mentioned, it is usually with horror. This is a healthy reaction, but those adverse to nationalisation must not spoil their case by overstating it. They should not speak as if the police were not already a semi-nationalised service; as if they had forgotten (as they perhaps conveniently have) that one-quarter of the police of England and Wales is controlled directly by the Home Secretary with no assistance from any local authority; as if police authorities had not lost to Whitehall many of the powers they possessed at one time. There are many reasons for this, but perhaps the most important is the existence and increasing influence of the Police Federation. The Federation is a national body which can speak for the members of all forces. It is almost always in favour of interference by the Secretary of State on all questions of pay and conditions of service, for it has found that he is usually more generous with taxpayers' money than police authorities are with ratepayers'. Unlike members of the public, therefore, the Federation has no reason to fear dictates from Whitehall. On the contrary, it constantly asks that the Home Secretary shall 'direct' a police authority or Chief Constable to do something on which the law gives them a discretion, e.g. to pay a pension in certain cases, to make up a man's pay whilst in the armed forces or to arrange duty hours in a certain way. Moreover, at a time of full employment outside the police and high wastage within it, the Federation is naturally in a strong position.

The opponents of nationalisation should not, therefore, idealise the present system by writing as if there were no central control of local police forces, and as if the Secretary of State did not on many matters communicate with the Chief Constable direct and not through his police authority. For instance, if the Government want the activities of a certain political party specially watched, they will not ask police authorities to instruct their Chief Constables to do so; Chief Constables will be communicated with direct, and most of them treat requests of this kind as orders. Nevertheless, complete nationalisation would make a difference, and it would be a change for the worse.

Similarly it is misleading to say that there is no secret police in this country. It is true in the sense that the names of all police officers can be discovered, but it is not true if we mean to imply that the police do not perform various activities secretly. They could not possibly perform the duties expected of them if they did not on occasion behave secretly, i.e. in plain clothes or incognito, or if they did not use secret methods for detecting crimes and watching suspects. Nor is it possible for members of police authorities or the public to discover what every police officer does.

The Police and the Public

In Great Britain to-day the police are, generally speaking, respected by the public. This has not always been so, except in the imagination of certain writers. We need not go as far as Mr. D. N. Pritt, who said in 1936 that 'the middle classes regard the police as well nigh perfect, whereas working class views on them are unprintable'; but it is important when considering this subject to keep sentiment under control. We can, nevertheless, confidently say that relations between the police and the public are better in Great Britain than in many other countries.

Why is this so? Here are some of the answers which have been given. 'The excellent relations which have always prevailed in this country between the police and the community are due in large measure to the fact that the police are drawn from the people and have as their duty to serve the people.' (Sir J. Anderson, in 1924, when Permanent Under Secretary of State at the Home Office— 'Public Administration,' Vol. III.) This does not get us very far, for it is difficult to see from whom the police could be drawn but the people, and many officials have as their duty 'to serve the people' but are not popular. Mr. Moylan gives a rather similar explanation: 'the police are the public and the public the police', ('Scotland Yard,' 1929). Mr. Reith, in his 'Short History of the British Police' (1948), makes the simpler point that the police are popular because they are kind and helpful. It is true that there is a long and splendid tradition of patience and courtesy in the British police, but this answer is not a completely satisfactory one, for it does not explain how the police can afford to be kind.

In accounting for the popularity of the British police the important fact is that the laws they enforce are by and large acceptable to the majority of the people. This in turn is due to two causes: firstly, the laws have been enacted by a democratic process, and, secondly, the police do not usually try to enforce unpopular or, as they sometimes term them, unenforceable laws, e.g. certain parts of the gaming laws. Some of the least popular laws at present, such as fuel and price controls are, it should be observed, enforced not by the police, but by special enforcement officers of the Ministries concerned. In other words, there is some truth in the saying that the police are popular because they are not too efficient. Another reason why relations between the police and the public are on the whole good is that the British are a law-abiding, easygoing, phlegmatic people, with a fairly high sense of social responsibility.

The 'Police State'

This good relationship between the police and the public is sometimes said to be the 'basic secret' of the success and efficiency of the British police (see, for instance, chapter XIX in Mr. Reith's 'Short History'). The Director of Public Prosecutions recently expressed a rather similar view when addressing Chief Constables. Speaking of the 'basic principles' which should govern the maintenance of the peace, he said that the most important one was that it is the right and duty of each individual citizen to help preserve law and order. He emphasised that it is to the private citizen that the police have to look for assistance, and his respect that they have to command, 'because with him lies the ultimate responsibility'. It is this principle, in the Director's view, which distinguishes the British conception of government from that of continental Europe. No one would deny that the task of the police is the easier the more law-abiding and co-operative are the people amongst whom they are to work, and indeed if no one ever broke the laws we could dispense with most of our policemen. But there are other important differences between this country and 'police states'. To mention only two: first, in a 'police state' the police are at the beck and call of the Executive Government. This is not so for five-sixths of the population of this country and could not be without a fundamental change in our system of police organisation. Recent trends towards larger police areas do not bring the 'police state' any nearer: on the contrary, the larger the area under the aegis of a local police authority, the more independent of central control it will probably be. Secondly, in a 'police state' the police normally have oppressive powers over individuals. They could, of course, be given such powers here without any change in our system of police organisation, but the Government would have no means of ensuring that they were used.

N 2

We conclude, therefore, that the organisation of our police service, though it has not deserved all the praise bestowed upon it and is still capable of improvement, yet does provide some substantial defences against tyranny.

Appendix

SUMMARY of Recommendations in Part II of the Oaksey Committee's Report on Police Conditions of Service (1949—Cmd. 7831) relating to negotiating machinery and arbitration.

1. The Police Council for England and Wales should be retained in very much its present form but should be called the Police Advisory Board. (A similar recommendation is made for Scotland.)

2. A new Police Council for Great Britain should be set up composed of an 'official side' and a 'staff side', and three independent members (one of whom would take the chair) appointed by the Lord Chancellor.

3. Certain subjects should be reserved for the new Police Council, and on some of the reserved subjects, including pay and the main conditions of service, the Council (and panels derived from it) should have executive powers of negotiation. On all other subjects its functions should be advisory and consultative.

4. On those subjects on which it has executive powers of negotiation, agreements reached by the Council should be binding on all parties subject to the overriding authority of Parliament.

5. Where the Council clearly fail to agree, the independent members should give a decision which should be similarly binding.

Index

ABERDEEN, 172, 176
Allen, Miss Mary, 133-4
Anderson, Sir J., 186
Amalgamation of police forces, 35-6, 53-5, 59-60, 61-8; in Scotland, 170, 172-3
Appeals, disciplinary, 39-40, 60, 76-8; in Scotland, 178
Association of Municipal Corporations, 19, 93
Astor, Lady, 136
Attorney General, 89
Audit, 81-2

BAIRD committee on policewomen, 135-7, 141
Blackstone, 25
Borough council, see Town council
Bow Street Patrols, 26
Bridgeman committee on policewomen, 136, 137, 141
British Union of Fascists, 47
Burgh Police (Scotland) Act (1892), 172

CHADWICK, Edwin, 30
Chief Constable, appointment of, 5, 72-6, 100; and central authority, 92-3, 130, 180-3, 185; complaints against, 87-8, 106-7; origins of, 161-3; and police authority, 95-8; powers of, (in boroughs) 110-2; 152-4, 159, 182-3; in Scotland, 176-7
Civil Defence Regions, see Regional Commissioners
Clerk to county council, 101
Clerk to police authority, 101
Clynes, Mr., 73, 137
Combined police authorities, 3-4, 5, 64-8, 98, 101
Commissioner of Police of Metropolis, 10, 27, 65, 103, 114-7, 120, 122
Constable, early history, 22-5, 28-30; office of, 10-4; rank of, 9, 158; in Scotland, 175; women as, 137-8
Controller and Auditor General, 119, 122
Cost of police, 7-8, 178
County and Borough Police Act (1856), 31-3, 36-7, 78, 79, 94
County boroughs, 2, 62
County council, 3, 43, 98-9, 101, 107-10; in Scotland, 171, 174, 176
County Councils Association, 19, 93
County Police Act (1839), 10, 31, 32, 169; rules made under, 31, 38, 72, 153, 162
Criminal Record Office, 117

DAMER-DAWSON, Miss, 133-4
Defence Regulations, 60-1, 144
Desborough committee, 12, 38, 41, 47, 53, 73, 110-1, 128, 135, 156, 170
Director of Public Prosecutions, 89-90, 187
Discipline, 5, 96, 105-6, 110-2; in Scotland, 176-7; and see Appeals, disciplinary
Dundee, 172, 174
Dunning, Sir L., 79, 139, 140

EDE, Mr. Chuter, 110
Edinburgh, 168, 172, 174

Enforcement officers of Ministries, 14–5, 187
Exchequer grant, 7, 36–8, 80–6; towards Metropolitan police force, 7, 118; in Scotland, 85, 178

FIELDING, brothers, 26
First Police Reserve, 8–9
Fisher v. Oldham Corporation, 11
Forensic Science Laboratories, 90–1
France, 27, 36–7

GEDDES committee, 71, 135
Glasgow, 168, 172, 174, 176
Greenock, 168, 172

HENDON police college, 116, 163–5
Higgins committee, 48
Home Office, see Home Secretary
Home Secretary, powers of, 5–6; regulations, 69–71; control over strengths, 71–2; over appointment of Chief Constable, 72–6; over Metropolitan police force, 114, 119–21, 130; responsibility to Parliament, 86–8; for Metropolitan police force, 121–3; and see Appeals; Chief Constable; Exchequer grant

IMPROVEMENT Commissioners, 26, 29; in Scotland, 168–9, 172
Inspectors of Constabulary, 6–7, 32–3, 78–80, 120–1, 144; in Scotland, 169

JOYNSON-HICKS, Sir W., 121, 124, 136–7
Justices of Peace, control over police, 23–4, 29–31, 103–5; and Standing Joint Committees, 3, 107–10

LOCAL Government Act (1888), 35, 43, 94, 104, 107
Local Government (Scotland) Act (1889), 170, 171
Local Government Boundary Commission, 54, 66–8
London, City of, 2, 7, 8, 26, 27, 78, 103; amalgamation with metropolitan police, 127–8
London County Council, 124–7
Lord Advocate, 170, 177

MAITLAND, 9, 13, 115, 124
Metropolitan Board of Works, 123
Metropolitan Police Act (1829), 10, 27, 118; (1839), 28, 127
Metropolitan police force, 1, 2, 27–8, 36, 62, 63, 113–31; promotion in, 159–60; women in, 134–7, 139, 145
Morrison, Mr. H., 18, 111
Moylan, Sir J., 12, 89, 121, 186
Municipal Corporations Act (1835), 29, 31–2, 123; (1882), 10, 94; (New Charters) Act (1877), 35

NATIONAL Service Act (1941), 57, 153
Nationalisation of police, 59, 63, 183–6
Non-county boroughs, 3, 53; loss of police forces, 62–5

OAKSEY committee, 16, 21, 49–53, 76, 107, 112, and Appendix

PARLIAMENT, 18, 86–8; and Metropolitan police, 121–3, 129
Peel, Sir R., 12, 27–8, 124, 127, 162
Police Act (1890), 45; (1909), 118; (1919), 15, 17, 19–20, 41–2, 69; (1946), 61–8, 85
Police authorities, 3–5, 94–102, 105, 107–12, 180–3; in Scotland, 174, 176–7
Police College, the national, 90–1, 164–7
Police Council, 19–21, 45, 69, 70, and Appendix; and policewomen, 141

Police (Expenses) Act (1874), 36
Police Federation, 15–21, 45, 48–9, 112, 163, 185; and policewomen, 142–3, 145
Police forces, 1–3, 34–5; in Scotland, 171
Police officers, 8–9; numbers of, 34; in Scotland, 171
Police pay, 38–9, 47–53, 69; of women, 141, 146–8
Police pensions, 39, 45, 52–3, 70–1
Police and public, 13, 186–7
Police ranks, 9
Police regulations, see Home Secretary
Police (Scotland) Act (1857), 169; (1946), 85, 173
Police strikes, 39–43
Police Union, 40–2
Police War Reserve, 8, 56–7
Policewomen, 132–51; in Scotland, 175
Political police, 117
Post-war committee, 61, 144
Pritt, Mr. D. N., 186
Promotion, 158–61; of women, 142; in Scotland, 178
Prosecutions, 88–90, 102; in Scotland, 177
Public Accounts Committee, 84–5, 119, 122

RECEIVER for Metropolitan police district, 118–9
Recruitment, 49–50, 152–5
Regional Commissioners, 57–9
Reith, Mr., 186, 187
Royal Commission on: County Police (1839), 30; Equal Pay (1946), 146–7; Local Government (1923), 54, 109; Local Taxation (1901), 37; Metropolitan Police (1908), 124; Police Powers and Procedure (1929), 46–7, 138–9

SAINT Helens, 97–8
Salford, 74–5
Samuel, Sir H., 180
Savidge, Miss, 46, 121
Scotland, 85, 88, 159, 168–79, and see under separate headings
Secret police, 185–6
Secretary of State, 2, 180–3, 185, and see Home Secretary
Secretary of State for Scotland, 168–9, 172, 173, 174
Select Committee of House of Commons on: Amalgamation of police forces (1932), 54–5; Amalgamation of Scottish police forces (1933), 170; County and Borough Police (1853), 32; Metropolitan police force (1833–4), 28
Shortt, Mr., 135
Simpson v. Dundee Corporation, 175
Special Constables, 9, 10, 44, 56, 105; in Scotland, 175
Standing Joint Committee, 3–5, 43, 98–9, 107–10

TOWN clerk, 101–2
Town council, 3, 99–101; in Scotland, 172, 174, 176
Trade Union Congress, 17–8, 40
Training of recruits, 90–1, 155–8; of women, 145–6; in Scotland, 178
Treasury, 84, 118, 125
Trenchard, Lord, 163–4

WATCH Committee, 3–5, 29, 99–101, 110–2, 159
Watchmen, 25, 26, 29
Wilson, Mr. C. H., 67
Women's Auxiliary Police Corps, 8, 56, 143

THE END

For Product Safety Concerns and Information please contact our EU
representative GPSR@taylorandfrancis.com
Taylor & Francis Verlag GmbH, Kaufingerstraße 24, 80331 München, Germany

www.ingramcontent.com/pod-product-compliance
Lightning Source LLC
Chambersburg PA
CBHW050443280326
41932CB00013BA/2219

* 9 7 8 1 0 3 2 4 1 8 0 5 6 *